2[illegible]AD

A History of Christianity

2159 AD

A History of Christianity

CRAIG BORLASE

Foreword by Maggi Dawn

DARTON · LONGMAN + TODD

To Evie, Barney, Bethany and Libby –
trusting that your own stories will weave in well with these.

First published in 2009 by
Darton, Longman and Todd Ltd
1 Spencer Court
140 – 142 Wandsworth High Street
London SW18 4JJ

ISBN: 978-0-232-52762-9

A catalogue record for this book is available from the British Library.

Designed and produced by Judy Linard.
Set in 11/14 point Bembo and Galahad Regular.
Printed and bound in Great Britain by Athenaeum Press, Gateshead, Tyne & Wear.

Contents

Acknowledgements		7
Foreword by Maggi Dawn		9
Introduction: The Siege of Jerusalem and the point of all this		11
1. 64 – 312:	Early Christianity	19
2. 313 – 476:	Church of the Roman Empire	41
3. 476 – 699:	The Early Middle Ages	61
4. 700 – 1499:	Too Much Time	71
5. 1399 – 1599:	Sex! Corpse! Incest! Pope! Torture!	91
6. 1521 – 1579:	Rolling out the Protestant Reformation	101
7. 1459 – 1769:	The World Gets Bigger	115
8. 1492 – 1769:	Ages of Reason and Awakenings	131
9. 1700 – 1851:	The Change	141
10. 1850 – 1944:	The Speed of Change	155
11. 1950 – 1983:	Rebuilding	167
12. 1984 – 2001:	A Cold Dawn	179

13. 2001 – 2019: The Storm Before the Calm 195
14. 2020 – 2062: The Age of Endings 209
15. 2049 – 2098: The Rise of the Tiger Theology 221
16. 2099 – 2133: Fresh Challenges in a Reworked World 233

Epilogue
2133 – : The End of the Beginning 247

A very selected bibliography 256

Acknowledgements

Thanks are due…

To the people who were kind enough to lend me their brains: Dr Stew Hotston, Craig Detweiler, Erwin McManus and Eric Bryant, Calum and Dr Abigail Macleod, the very good Dr Kent Barshov, Terry Glaspey, the Rev Chris Russell, Ben Niblet. Thank you for meeting me half way down the mountain.

To the friends who lent me their shoulders: Charles and Janet Morris, Chris and Belinda, Juliette, the Buchanans, Young Craig, Cathy, Vincent, Liam and Andy, Jona Skipper, the Nivens, Mizzie and Ian. Thank you for speaking and listening.

To the church I belong to: the community of Saint Laurence, Reading and friends at Soul Survivor and Tearfund. Thank you for committing to something worth sharing in.

To the family who breathe life into all of this: the beautiful Emma, the inspiring Evie, the upstanding Ba, the delightful Bessie and the freshly-arrived-but-hugely-loved Libby.

To the publishers: thank you to the team at DLT, with particular gratitude to David Moloney for being there from the very beginning.

To everything else that inspired me while writing: the music of Jason Upton, Bon Iver, Jon Foreman, Amadou and Mariam, Tumbling Ground by the Black Peppercorns. The sight and smell of a 3 x 4 log cabin on a late winter's evening. The voices of Brennan Manning, Rob Bell and Eugene Peterson. My mother's fountain pen and bible. The thought of a summer in France. The river Thames, Whiteknights Lake and Solva, Pembrokeshire. National Geographic features and the prose of Sebastian Faulks.

Foreword

It was recently reported in the national press that there was a dramatic drop in the number of students choosing to pursue history as an academic subject. In a culture ever more seduced by the present moment, history and tradition seem to be losing currency. But to fail to know and interpret our history affects every part of life, not least our understanding of the Church and the Christian faith.

It's common in Church circles, when a tradition has grown stale or lost its integrity, for people to say that we should 'return' to the faith of the early church, as if we could simply leap back over two millennia of history to rediscover the beliefs and practices of the New Testament era and start afresh from there. But such a leap is an impossibility, not only because we cannot know in any kind of detail what the first century Church really looked like, but also because our understanding of the New Testament Church is filtered through two millennia of Christian history that have occurred in the meantime. We cannot separate our interpretation of the New Testament from the layers of history we have inherited, any more than we can turn lemonade back into lemons, sugar and water. The idea that we could dispense with history and begin again is a fallacy, and it's even more mistaken to think we could avoid the mistakes of history by dissociating ourselves from them. In the famous, though often misquoted, words of Spanish philosopher George Santayana, 'Those who cannot remember the past are condemned to repeat it.'

The real solution to an unsatisfying, often embarrassing and sometimes baffling tradition is to learn about where we've come from in order to know how to shape the future. By knowing and accepting our own history, we gain a clearer understanding of why things are the way they are now; in terms of liturgy, theology and church practice we save ourselves from reinventing the wheel over and over again, and we also stand a much better chance of steering our own future in an informed way.

2159AD is an introduction to the history of the Church, a whistlestop tour through twenty centuries of Church development, stopping along the way at the major events to examine why events happened as they did, and what effect they had on the unfolding story of the Church. But Craig Borlase gives us Church history with a twist by telling his story from an imagined position a century and a half into the future. He views the present as if it were already history, and in doing so gives his idea of what the Church could be like in the future, with visions to embrace and dangers to avoid.

Constructing a vision of the future would be pointless if it were merely an attempt to predict what happens next. There's little purpose or benefit in being history's fortune teller. But there's every reason, as Coleridge believed, to picture what might be possible in order to imagine a better world into being in the present. By giving us an account of history from a fictitious future perspective, 2159AD reminds us that all we are now will one day be read as someone else's history, and considers the lessons of the past with an eye to what we might yet become. It lays a challenge at our door – not only to know about where we've come from, but to become more aware that the way we live out our faith now is creating a spiritual legacy for future generations.

Maggi Dawn, Cambridge, 2009

Introduction

The Siege of Jerusalem and the point of all this

My knowledge of the history of Christianity is shocking. I suppose I know the basics well enough to be able to tell my Peter from my Paul, but once we get out of the New Testament with its stories of martyrs' stonings and divinely-assisted jail-breaks I find myself having considerable difficulty. I know that something major happened when a Roman emperor saw the light, but after that wasn't it nothing more than endless years of witch hunts and strange men with even stranger beards? I know that Calvin was someone important, but I'm not all that sure if I'm actually a Calvinist myself, or even whether I should want to be one in the first place. Move forward a while and I'm still struggling; did the Church stay as silent as it appears that it did during the Second World War? Was there really quite so much fuss made over the ordination of women and gays? And how come it took Christians so long to wake up to the problem with the planet?

I don't know if I can work it all out, but something gnaws at me telling me it's worth a try.

Before we start, though, I'm wondering if there are a few things to clear up, like understanding what makes all this stuff important anyway? Why should I care? And why is it that someone like me, a Christian for all his life, can have got so far and yet know so little about the ancestors that wept, fought, raged, died, argued and prayed this faith into what it is today?

I've been thinking about that. I grew up in a church that was insular and single-minded. Boil it down to its absolute essence and the message that came down from the stage and screens was clear; why bother looking back when the future was so close at hand? We weren't necessarily Rapturists, although I'm sure there were a few among us, searching the skies for interesting cloud formations. Yet we were all encouraged to believe that Jesus was coming back soon. Very soon.

I don't know why this meant that our history mattered less. Perhaps we were worried that the Lord might take offence if we appeared too smart on our first meeting. Maybe we really did think that we'd got it right; all those centuries that had passed before us were merely a warm up to this, to us; the final act before the curtain fell. Or could it be that we just thought it was all too tedious to warrant further study?

'The trouble with studying history,' commented a scholar some time back in the time before terrorstrikes, bombs and floods, 'is that all of it has already happened and that most of it should never have happened in the first place.'

Perhaps this is why we're shy of it today. Could it be that, like a lot of families, we don't really like a whole lot of our ancestors? Have we hoped that if we ignore them we might be able to get away from the worst ones? If we don't ever mention their names or their crimes, will nobody ever guess that we are related?

I've thought hard about it but these really are the only two reasons I can come up with for the knowledge gap. Arrogance or foolishness. It's not much of an upbringing is it?

Other questions need an answer too; why bother now?

In spite of the fact that I've moved on from belonging to the type of churches that preach the immanence of the apocalypse, I'm feeling the pull towards new directions, the sort I've never previously really noticed. While there's a fever for predicting the end of the world, I'm adopting something other than my usual silent disdain. I'm starting to wonder whether we're the only ones who have ever felt this way or if the beginning of the end has been glimpsed before. Are we unique or are we locked onto a course that has been travelled many, many times over already?

And why should I care? In spite of the borders and the authorities and the fact that you can't even seem to be able to buy a cup of coffee these days without having to prove your identity in a hundred different ways, one thing is clear: we're living in unusual times. The Church is split; by geography, theology, values, purpose. Has it always been this way? Was it ever the same? Or better? Worse?

My grandfather used to occasionally talk about 'kicking the tyres'. We'd always have to look surprised when he said it, and sit back and listen to his explanation, all wide-eyed and freshly amazed:

'It was something we used to do to cars,' he'd start, and at the word 'cars' we'd all snigger on cue but then go silent again when he pretended to get offended. 'Whenever a friend had a new one we'd always go out and kick the soft bit round the wheels. You could tell a lot about how a car had been looked after from the kicking the tyres.'

That would be it; our part in the game over, Granddad would now go off on some other drift about the faded past.

Thinking about it now, I suppose that's what I want to do with this, to kick the tyres beneath the Church. I want to see if I can find out where it's been, how it's been looked after, and much longer it's got left.

THREADS

I do know one bit of Church history. Even before I access the archives I can start with this: the Siege of Jerusalem. Then again, who doesn't know this story? Ever since the bombs went off in 2062 we've all known about the first time that the apocalypse paid a visit to the Holy Land.

It was not long after Jesus had been crucified, returned to his followers for a few weeks and then disappeared again. A few years had passed and Palestine remained occupied by the Romans. For a while they slackened their grip on the leash, allowing Herod Agrippa I (who happened to be the grandson of Herod the Great) to assume a little more control. He did this in a number of ways, one notable example being his decision to have James, the brother of John, executed. And then he imprisoned Peter, intending to kill him too. But God did his thing with an angel and Peter was set free (you can read this for yourself in the Book of the Acts 12:6–10 if you like).

After Agrippa was struck down by God for being so arrogant as to suggest that he and the Almighty were on the same pay level, the Romans took a little more interest in restoring and maintaining order in the region. This, however, did not go down altogether well among the Jews, and in AD 66 they started to speak out against Roman rule. There were fights over money. The Romans were demanding too high a figure for taxes and the Jews throughout the area were starting to revolt.

Rome responded with further measures to control the people. As was the custom, reactionaries when caught ran the risk of being crucified. Throughout Palestine the Roman forces marched, attacking and quietening their grumbling, dangerous Jewish subjects. Jerusalem had long been an impressive and important city, and since Herod the Great had created such a magnificent second temple (the first one being destroyed by the Nebuchadrezzar II and the Babylonians in 587 BC) the city's gravitational pull had gained in strength. When Passover came around in the year AD 70, as many as three million pilgrims approached the city to join in the celebrations of their freedom from slavery.

Ironically, the 30,000 Roman soldiers that the travellers had passed on their way into the city had a different set of ideas about the nature of Jewish freedom. The soldiers had Jerusalem surrounded and while they allowed the three million pilgrims to enter, by the time they came to leave, the Romans simply refused to let them go.

For 143 days Jerusalem was under siege. With such drastically increased numbers in the city, water and food resources were pushed beyond their limits. Within the walls, chaos reigned. People starved, disease spread, violence errupted. Factions fought against each other and, according to the historian Josephus, some individuals even resorted to cannibalism. All the Roman soldiers had to do was sit outside the walls and wait.

After six months of murder, starvation and populist rule gone badly wrong, the Romans built siege towers against the walls and stoned the Temple Mount.

There is some disagreement about what happened next. Some suggest that Titus – the military commander – led the charge and encouraged the decimation of the city. I prefer the other version, the one that has him shouting and waving and desperately trying to get his soldiers to put out the fire that had started around the temple. Titus had meant to turn the place from a Jewish holy site into a temple for worship of any number of pagan gods. But he was too late. The fires devoured the buildings and his soldiers charged ahead, fueled by a crazed passion for blood.

Josephus continues:

> 'Most of the victims were peaceful citizens, weak, and unarmed, butchered wherever they were caught. Around the Altar the heap of corpses grew higher and higher, while down the Sanctuary steps poured a river of blood and the bodies of those killed at the top slithered to the bottom. The soldiers were like men possessed and there was no holding them, nor was there any arguing with the fire. Caesar therefore led his staff inside the building and viewed the Holy Place of the sanctuary with its furnishings, which went far beyond the accounts circulating in foreign countries, and fully justified their splendid reputation in our own.'
>
> Flavius Josephus, War of the Jews, Book VI, Chapter IV

As many as one million Jews were murdered, with almost 100,000 captured and used as entertainment in circus rings around the empire; presumably they ended up dying to the sound of slow applause and easy ridicule. Others escaped; like the Christians led by Jesus' cousin, Symeon. Before the siege began they remembered the words that Jesus had spoken forty years earlier: he'd told them about the suffering that was to come, about escaping to the mountains and the destruction of the Temple. As he led his fellow Christians out and up to the hill town of Pella, Symeon must have wondered about the fate of the city.

Everybody knew that this was a mighty defeat, but they also knew that the story was built out of more significant elements than a stronger army crushing a weakened people. Even Titus could see it; refusing to accept a wreath of victory, as there was 'no merit in vanquishing people forsaken by their own God'.

Was this the judgement that Jesus was speaking about forty years earlier? Was this the promised end?

These days people are wondering the same thing as they were back in AD 70; is there judgment in the air, are things moving towards something... eternal? Of course, Jerusalem doesn't really exist any more – there's barely anything left of the stones that had stood for so long. But there is talk of the end.

More than two thousand years of history joins that moment when Jerusalem fell for the second time to this. All those years must have been characterised by something, but what? Years of hate, years of death, years of sacrifice? I suppose that somewhere within the story of Christianity are the threads that weave together to begin to make an image of what Jesus meant when he talked about the Church as his own bride. Somehow, by looking back, I want to see if I can find it; that essence of whatever it was that we were supposed to be. I want to trace the threads and find the brilliance that has been hidden by apathy, ignorance or too many years spent chasing after the wrong goals. And I want to be wrong.

CB

February 14th, 2159

Chapter One

64 – 312
Early Christianity

PERSECUTION

Some say that it burned for five days, others say seven. Some say that it destroyed four of the city's districts, others say fourteen. But all agree that Rome's Great Fire of AD 64 was the start of something different. For Nero Claudius Caesar Augustus Germanicus – ten years into his reign and fresh from a successful suppression of the British revolt – it was the perfect excuse to flex his muscles at home. For his Roman opponents the fire was the ideal opportunity to char Nero's name with accusations of neglect and frivolity. For the growing number of Christians, the fire was a precursor to one thing: persecution.

The flames started on the night of 18 July, AD 64, somewhere around the shops that clustered like limpets to the city's entertainment mecca – the *circus maximus*. With a capacity of 250,000 the hippodrome supported a colossal number of small businesses, spewing out hoards of potential customers during chariot races. On that particular Saturday night, though, they choked on fire, not crowds.

The blaze devastated homes and businesses. We do not know how many lives it claimed at the time, yet the stories that surround its impact are still told today. Nero, it is said, fiddled while Rome burned. Technically it would have to have been a lyre – what with fiddles not being invented for another thousand years – but why let the facts get in the way of a good story? It's alleged that on hearing news of the fire the emperor dressed up in stage clothes and sang a lost epic that retold the entire Trojan war in intricate detail. What's

28 – 75
Buddhism enters
Emperor Ming's China

64
Nero's Rome burns

c67
Peter martyred

70
Siege of Jerusalem

more bizarre than the story itself is the fact that for over 2,000 years this account has been held to be true.

What we do know for sure – thanks to contemporary historian Tacitus – is that Nero was 30 miles south in the city of Antium on the night in question. Later he returned to the city, surveyed the damage to his palace as well as other buildings and used his own funds to start a significant relief effort. Food was distributed and shelter provided to those in need and an ambitious new urban development plan drawn up.

Nero understood Roman mobs. A shrewd and gifted leader – not born into the role, but like many of his kind adopted and elevated to the position – his influence had grown in the ten years since he came to power, aged just 16. He had neutered the Senate, murdered his mother and instigated policies that pleased the lower classes at the expense of the wealthy.

So the decision to find someone to blame for the fire was a necessary one. Even though there was no clear evidence that the fire was started deliberately – and further accidental fires went on to harm the city in AD 69 and AD 80 - rumours abounded. Nero's enemies whispered that it was in fact the Emperor himself who ordered the flames. Of course Nero had to hit back at the accusers and do something that would win over the opinions of the masses, at least to distract them from such gossip. Forget the truth; perception mattered more.

But who to blame?

The Christians made an ideal target. They were a minority, yet a growing one. They had few friends yet numerous enemies. What's

c80
Rome's Colosseum completed

138
Hadrian's Wall completed in Britain

166 – 167
Plague in Roman Empire

235 – 284
Civil war in Roman Empire

more, they seemed to have a thing for persecution. It was in their genes. Tacitus – aged just nine at the time of the fire – later recalled in his work 'Annals' (translated by Church and Brodribb) Nero's methods of quashing the conspiracy theories about his own involvement:

> Consequently, to get rid of the report, Nero fastened the guilt and inflicted the most exquisite tortures on a class hated for their abominations, called Christians by the populace. Christus, from whom the name had its origin, suffered the extreme penalty during the reign of Tiberius at the hands of one of our procurators, Pontius Pilatus, and a most mischievous superstition, thus checked for the moment, again broke out not only in Judaea, the first source of the evil, but even in Rome, where all things hideous and shameful from every part of the world find their centre and become popular. Accordingly, an arrest was first made of all who pleaded guilty; then, upon their information, an immense multitude was convicted, not so much of the crime of firing the city, as of hatred against mankind. Mockery of every sort was added to their deaths. Covered with the skins of beasts, they were torn by dogs and perished, or were nailed to crosses, or were doomed to the flames and burnt, to serve as a nightly illumination, when daylight had expired.

And so the persecution took on a new form. While the decision to crucify Jesus was a political and theological one, Nero started to

28 – 75
Buddhism enters
Emperor Ming's China

64
Nero's Rome burns

c67
Peter martyred

70
Siege of Jerusalem

murder Christians because it was both convenient and entertaining. For both Nero and the Jews it was clear that Christians and the Christ they followed were a threat to their power. Christians were no longer persecuted because they were hated, but because their deaths were useful; an event in themselves. In fact, the entertainment that flowed from their killing was of such high standard that Nero took to dressing up as a charioteer as he wandered among the crowds that marvelled at the human torches illuminating dark Roman skies.

Starting with the crucifixion of Jesus and ending with the co-opting of Christianity by Constantine in 313, Christians were actively persecuted by Rome as often as they were not. Not all Emperors went out of their way to discriminate against them, but between the twelve that did, the death toll rose with every passing year.

Of course, it was not only the Romans who found the death of Christians to be good for business. Jewish leaders continued to cheer on the suppression of Christianity. Yet while there was ample evidence of Jewish-backed persecution throughout the Apostolic period – as narrated by the book of Acts – it appears that by the time Nero developed his own policy of being cruel and unusual by using crucified corpses as candles for garden parties, there were far fewer Jewish leaders actively persecuting Christians themselves.

One of the last incidents is the death of James the Just – sometimes known as James the Less. Bishop of Jerusalem - who some would argue was the author of the New Testament book of James and

c80
Rome's Colosseum completed

138
Hadrian's Wall completed in Britain

166 – 167
Plague in Roman Empire

235 – 284
Civil war in Roman Empire

was thought to be one of the original seventy disciples of Jesus – James somehow fell foul of the High Priest Ananaus Ben Ananus. Ananus encouraged the Sanhedrin to have James stoned to death, a decision which eventually backfired. After James's killing the new Roman governor decided that it was a step too far and had the High Priest deposed.

A pattern began to emerge: instead of carrying out the deeds themselves, Jewish leaders encouraged their Roman rulers to do it for them. After all, with rulers like Nero having a fierce appetite for acts of shocking violence it became far more effective to whisper accusations into the ears of those in power rather than try to take control of the reins oneself.

We can see this same pattern in play a century after Ananus and Nero were at work. Smyrna (now Izmir modern day Turkey) was home to Polycarp, the local bishop. As part of the annual celebrations that honoured the Roman leaders, crowds gathered to see yet more Christians killed by wild beasts. Yet the audience was jaded. They'd seen it all before. 'Away with the atheists,' they shouted – a common term for Christians at the time – 'go and find Polycarp.' The bishop was duly found. Old, but full of faith, he spent the final two hours before his arrest giving prayerful thanks to God.

The events that followed have been retold over the centuries. Brought in front of the local proconsul, Polycarp was offered a deal: repent of his faith or die. The 86 year-old was witty and courageous, attempting a little last minute evangelism of the Roman leader. When the crowd heard that he had refused to recant they called for

28 – 75
Buddhism enters
Emperor Ming's China

64
Nero's Rome burns

c67
Peter martyred

70
Siege of Jerusalem

him to be put in a ring with a lion. Impossible, said the proconsul, for the games season was over. So the Jews in the mob performed their usual role and brought timber to build a pyre. Polycarp persuaded them to not nail him to the stake, knowing that his faith was far stronger than the temptation to flee. Quickly the flames surrounded him like a ship's sail. Yet something was not quite right: something looked a little different. It seemed that he was burning without actually burning up, as if the raging fire was not touching him at all. So the mob intervened and had the ageing bishop stabbed. Bizarrely, the crowd was able to see how from the wound there came so much blood that the fire was extinguished. To the crowd's amazement a dove appeared to leave the bishop's body and fly upwards.

BEHIND CLOSED DOORS AND UNDERGROUND

As the death count grew, so too did the numbers of Jews and non-Jews joining the Christian sect – this small yet potentially explosive band of believers. Origen – recognised by some as the first fully-fledged theologian, although Paul and Jesus offer pretty stiff competition for the title – commented in the middle of the third century on 'the multitude of people coming to faith', while another writer at the time explained that numbers 'day by day increase more and more'.

By the end of the first century – and not more than seventy years after Christ's handful of followers were told to get on with the job of making disciples – there were as many as one million Christians spread across the Roman empire. The growth was significant, and for

c80
Rome's Colosseum completed

138
Hadrian's Wall completed in Britain

166 – 167
Plague in Roman Empire

235 – 284
Civil war in Roman Empire

today's observer the increase in numbers appears to be linked to the increase in persecution. A couple of centuries later, as Christianity prepared to be adopted as the religion of choice for Roman Emperor Constantine, between five and twenty-five per cent of the Empire's population proclaimed – albeit with a certain degree of fear when doing so in public – their Christian faith. Within another three centuries some estimates suggest that 40 million people counted themselves as Christians – almost a quarter of the world's population.

But it is the early period of the faith – the one marked on one side by the death, resurrection and ascension of Jesus and Constantine's single-handed creation of Christendom on the other – that concerns us. Just how was it that they managed to achieve such growth while remaining an underground – and sometimes violently and extensively persecuted – movement? How did this sect of Judaism evolve into the early Church at all?

What was the early Church like? Laying down a clear blueprint for their activities is a little more complicated than you might think. The lack of formal structure or Operator's Manual, as well as the theological conviction behind the faith meant that groups of believers interpreted and expressed their faith in ways which made sense to their immediate surroundings – as Paul's letters throughout the New Testament make clear. In fact any attempt at defining the early Church needs to start by going negative; focusing in on the elements that we know to be absent for large numbers of believers.

They didn't have public buildings. Instead they met in houses,

28 – 75
Buddhism enters
Emperor Ming's China

64
Nero's Rome burns

c67
Peter martyred

70
Siege of Jerusalem

choosing to modify their homes by knocking down the odd wall to accommodate increasing numbers. While we can see it in evidence in the book of Acts, long after the time the last eyewitnesses to Christ had died off public preaching was simply too dangerous and praying for others to convert was rare. Instead, intercession was dominated by the theme of grace for their enemies. As for evangelism, there is little mention of it in original texts. The North African Bishop – and eventual martyr – Cyprian, compiled a list of 120 instructions to help establish a sound Christian faith. Evangelism simply didn't feature. Perhaps it was at best the 121st most important element of Christianity, but even this form of optimism puts the early Church at stark odds with the forms into which it would evolve.

Worship was hardly attractive either; if you were a pagan you were simply refused admission. The doors were shut and, from the mid-first century onwards the only way of opening them was by making a colossal commitment of time, energy and trust and signing up to become a *catechumen*. These students of the faith were trained towards the ultimate goal, baptism into the Christian faith, but not without considerable sacrifice on their own part.

Throughout their training – which lasted at least three years – any catechumen would take part in daily lessons which would have them exploring, absorbing and understanding the impact of Christ's life, death and resurrection. This rabbinical pattern of study and discussion, passing on wisdom from one to another was as laborious as it was essential. Students were regularly exorcised; they were expected to behave with integrity and honour and were asked to leave every service as soon as the biblical reading and teaching were over. It was only after baptism – with its three-day long preparation of exorcisms, fasting and fully naked submersions overseen by a fully naked priest in a river on Easter Sunday at dawn – that they truly belonged. It was only then that they were allowed to join in with prayer, the kiss of peace and share in the Eucharistic meal of bread and wine. So baptism was never seen as a single event, just as Christianity itself was not seen as a service or meeting. The process of becoming a member of the Church unfolded over a long period of time, the Church nurturing her growing infants just as a mother grows her young. Finally, emerging from the waters, the former catechist would fill their lungs with fresh air and let out the cry 'I believe'. New life was finally theirs.

Caecillus – a contemporary (and sceptical) writer – wondered why it was that Christians 'never speak in public, never meet in the open, if it not be that the aspect of their worship is either criminal or shameful?'

The answer requires a less rigid mind than Caecillus's; Christianity was an underground affair not because their practices were abhorrent or deviant. They were hidden from public view because Nero's persecutions put an end to the pursuit of Paul's advice to the Church in Corinth to integrate. They were underground because – by their own admission – they were *paroikoi*: resident aliens, the sort described in 1 Peter as strangers living here in 'reverent fear'. They had shifted away because theirs was a viral revolution, a relational, personal phenomenon that did not require big platforms or political support

28 – 75
Buddhism enters
Emperor Ming's China

c67
Peter martyred

64
Nero's Rome burns

70
Siege of Jerusalem

to prosper. They were underground because it was the most effective place to be.

If there was one central text that the early Church revolved around, it was Christ's instruction to 'love your enemies'. Such love not only dictated how they responded to those who opposed and persecuted them, it also defined and united their communities. Lending a clear identity, this attitude informed more than their rituals and roles, it defined their very essence; their relationships.

HOW DID THEY GROW?

Person by person, the faith grew. Each conversation whispered at work or to a neighbour in a darkened hallway was another small step towards Christianity's remarkable advance. It may have lacked what subsequent generations would identify as *evangelism*, but this early Church had something that would be missing for centuries to come; an understanding that relationships with those outside the faith were a far more valuable currency than public preaching or political influence.

Caecillus liked writing about Christians. As well as wondering about the nature of those private meetings, he commented that Christians were 'silent in public, chattering in corners'. Gradually those corner-conversations grew into friendships, and those in turn developed bonds of trust between the people. And when crisis or difficulty hit, Christians often found themselves to be the first to be called to for help.

The early Church helped people – its success is perhaps found in a statement as simple as that. Everyone who belonged was

c80
Rome's Colosseum completed

138
Hadrian's Wall completed in Britain

166 – 167
Plague in Roman Empire

235 – 284
Civil war in Roman Empire

called upon to make sacrifices and it was their sense of community that determined their influence in the world around them. Financial support was a cornerstone of membership, with wealthier Christians giving through the Church's common fund to poorer members. In this way the usual divisions of society were torn down, making way for a way of life that acted on Christ's instructions.

Christians buried people. This was more significant than might first appear, since their willingness to touch dead bodies and even bury them was at odds with much of the dominant culture. While the Roman dead were left in a necropolis (the word taken from the Greek from Greek *nekropolis* meaning 'city of the dead'), Christians laid the departed in a cemetery, the word translated directly from the Greek as 'sleeping place'. Christians simply saw death differently. They cared for the graves of those now dead, they were kind to strangers and supported the poor from wherever they came. As one of the earliest recorded Christian apologists writing in Latin, Minucius Felix had an interested perspective on the impact of believers, how their 'beauty of life causes strangers to join the ranks … We do not talk about great things; we live them.'

Everything was shared. Not that private property was abolished; it wasn't. But these people lived free from the insecurities that led others to hoard away possessions. After all, why fill your life with status symbols when your ultimate status as a follower of Christ and child of God was so far beyond doubt that you would even give your life for its cause?

28 – 75
Buddhism enters
Emperor Ming's China

64
Nero's Rome burns

c67
Peter martyred

70
Siege of Jerusalem

As well as challenging previously held assumptions that both the wealthy and the outcast should remain in their respective positions, the early Church began to reconfigure notions of death as the end of the affair – hence the transformation from the *city of the dead* to a *place of sleeping*. It became common to celebrate the life of a martyr either on the anniversary of their birth, or their death – for it was the point at which their lives continued eternally.

Nothing spreads a message quite like martyrdom, as Tertullian highlighted with his observation that 'the blood of the martyrs is the seed of the Church'. Those early Christians who followed Jesus' lead ended up crucified, burnt at the stake or ripped apart by lions while the voyeurs cheered from the banks of tiered seating. But the means by which their bodies were broken matters far less than the pages they added to the story of sacrifice.

It might have been for something as incendiary as daring to preach in public, but in AD 107 Ignatius was sentenced to be killed by beasts. On the 1,500 mile journey from Antioch to Rome Ignatius wrote a series of letters, reflecting on what had passed and what was to come. To his fellow believers in Rome he urged that they might 'allow me to follow the example of the suffering of my God'.

The connection between Christ's death and the fate of the martyr was as powerful as it was simple. Polycarp understood the importance of holding onto his beliefs in his final hours, while fellow martyr Pionius commented that he was 'not rushing towards death, but towards life'. Tertullian – a phenomenal scholar of the early Church

c80
Rome's Colosseum completed

138
Hadrian's Wall completed in Britain

166 – 167
Plague in Roman Empire

235 – 284
Civil war in
Roman Empire

– commented that 'no one would want to be killed unless possessed of the truth'.

Yet not everyone agreed. Tertullian frequently locked horns with those who saw martyrdom as being of rather less importance. Gnosticism – the belief that humans inhabit an imperfect world created by an imperfect god – latched onto Christianity and found converts. Those who signed up felt that true Christian witness was found not in death but knowledge (*gnosis*). For those who would rather not lose their lives for the sake of their beliefs this had a certain appeal. Furthermore, gnostic Christians claimed that God's transcendent glory meant that involvement in pagan sacrifice could not touch the believer. In other words, they could pretty much do what they wanted with their bodies as long as their minds were getting a rigorous workout.

As the early Church grew and the end of the third century approached, persecutions increased. Emperor Diocletian launched a decade's worth of intense witch hunts in AD 303 as the 'baptism of blood' increased.

But not everyone wanted to become a martyr. In Antioch many Christians gave in to the pressure and took part in public sacrifices to Roman gods. Romanus – a visiting Christian from Palestine – saw the one-time faithful joining in with the crowds on their way to sacrifice. His shock and horror led him to try to stop the procession. For his pains he was executed, dying in defence of Christian integrity.

In the years to come the Church would have to find a way of dealing with those who gave in to the pressure from their persecu-

28 – 75
Buddhism enters
Emperor Ming's China

c67
Peter martyred

64
Nero's Rome burns

70
Siege of Jerusalem

tors; should – and how could – they be reintegrated into the Church community? After such a premium had been placed on sacrifice and shared experience, how could the gulf between the memory of the martyrs and the presence of defectors every hope to be bridged? This would not just be relevant in the coming decades, but down throughout history. In 1556 Thomas Cramner would pay with his life for switching sides while five hundred years later tensions between Christians and Hindus in India would create a similar environment.

THOUGHT

Origen did not get to be a martyr. Yet this was not through weakness – at least, not quite. Eventually this young man would become known as the Unbreakable One, the Iron Man, perhaps the first theologian who brought to Christianity the powers of intellectual rigour and respectability.

He was born in AD 185 in Alexandria, today the second largest city on Egypt. With Africa at its back and the Mediterranean to its front the city held one of the seven wonders of the world, the Pharos Lighthouse. Alexandria was also home to one of the world's greatest ever libraries and the epicentre of philosophical debate and intellectual progress. It gave birth to the Greek as well as the Coptic Orthodox Churches of Alexandria. While both may be a little quiet these days, their continuing presence allows them to lay claim to having the deepest roots of all the Christian Churches. Today – as ever – they seem little troubled by progress or seem to have no need to reform or react to the changes beyond their ornate walls.

c80
Rome's Colosseum completed

138
Hadrian's Wall completed in Britain

166 – 167
Plague in Roman Empire

235 – 284
Civil war in Roman Empire

As the God they serve is above and beyond, so too do they continue to walk the ancient paths that have been followed since Christianity's birth.

Young Origen was also remarkable. Bright and full of faith, his father, Leonides, pressed him to recite Scripture daily. When eventually Leonides was arrested for his beliefs, the seventeen-year-old Origen wrote him a letter. He told his father that he should not give in to the pressure to recant his faith out of fear for his family. His death, Origen assured, would not be in vain.

It wasn't. And in fact, Origen himself wanted to follow his father's lead, yet when the opportunity arose to join a public demonstration that would clearly have led to arrest and possible execution, Origen's mother hid the young man's clothes. Seventeen-year-olds being notoriously self-conscious, Origen opted to remain inside. He may have been ready to give up his life for his faith, but his dignity was another matter altogether.

Yet Origen went on to become one of the founding fathers of the early Church. In spite of the fact that barely any of his original work survived, his writings were often quoted by others and it is possible to build up a clear picture of his passions and positions. While it may appear that Origen and the Gnostics shared the opinion that knowledge was a goal worth pursuing, Origen differed with his assumption that the truth could be found within Scripture itself. It was to that task that he applied himself fully throughout his life.

Origen was not always wise when it came to Scripture. As a young man he had a little trouble with Matthew 19:12 ('For some

28 – 75
Buddhism enters
Emperor Ming's China

c67
Peter martyred

64
Nero's Rome burns

70
Siege of Jerusalem

are eunuchs because they were born that way; others were made that way by men; and others have renounced marriage because of the kingdom of heaven. The one who can accept this should accept it.'). The young scholar worried about falling into sin by teaching females, and therefore – rumour has it – made himself a eunuch. Whether by drugs or a minor operation we cannot be sure, but we do know that self emasculation was illegal as well as popular.

Years later, however, Origen would write that the passage should most certainly not be taken literally. We can only wonder if he was wincing as he transferred the words to the page.

In spite of so little of his work surviving in the original, Origen's contribution to the legacy of Christianity was immense. His work demanded that Scripture be approached with intellect intact. The passages that were deemed impossible to understand – or to be taken as anything other than literal truth – were, according to Origen, proud owners of a deeper meaning. Allegory was an essential device to grasp, and though he was criticised for putting his own ideas onto the text, his approach has held power at various points throughout history. After all, Homer did it, so did Plato, and much of the latter days of the twentieth century followed suit. Today, I wonder whether we need a return to this sort of discipline?

Origen taught about the character of God. Where Scripture depicts a God with emotions, Origen struggled to take these notions literally. He claimed that God must not be thought of as any kind of body, nor to exist in a body; an approach that would evolve over the centuries – with mixed results.

c80
Rome's Colosseum completed

138
Hadrian's Wall completed in Britain

166 – 167
Plague in Roman Empire

235 – 284
Civil war in Roman Empire

The years of teaching brought recognition, acolytes and rivals. Eventually – as Emperor Decius assumed power in AD 249 – the first wave of persecution in fifty years started up. Many of Origen's pupils were imprisoned and martyred and Origen himself was arrested, imprisoned and tortured in an effort to force him to recant, yet he would not break. After all, he was the Iron Man. Eventually he was released, faith intact, but body broken. His final five years were spent, appropriately enough, in obscurity, yet his legacy strengthened the Church for generations to come.

Years earlier Justin – an early writer and martyr – captured the essence of the Church's early success; 'the Christian's god is not circumscribed by place; invisible, he fills the heavens and the earth, and he is worshipped and glorified by believers everywhere.'

The early Church was fluid, dynamic and inspired to make bold changes and grand gestures. During the first century Christians made a significant change to their meetings. Instead of continuing the Jewish tradition of meeting on a Saturday, their main gatherings started to take place on a Sunday. For the Jews this made little sense at all; why shift the Sabbath day from its traditional position at what was commonly regarded as the end of the week? Why stop imitating God who – as the Genesis story reminds us – also rested at the end of the first week? For the Christians, however, the choice of Sunday as Sabbath was deliberate and full of meaning. To meet on the symbolic first day of the week aligned the Church with God's transformation of the darkness, with the very start of his creation, as it bound them in to the day on which Christ rose from the dead, and it is clear that

28 – 75
Buddhism enters
Emperor Ming's China

c67
Peter martyred

64
Nero's Rome burns

70
Siege of Jerusalem

the early Church placed transformation at the very heart of their beliefs.

They found life in death. Meeting together at cemeteries was not unusual. These special religious activities helped continue a relationship with those that had died, and often on the anniversary of their birth – or death – believers would gather at the tomb of a departed loved one and share a ritual meal at the graveside. Fish, bread, cakes and wine that was poured over the tomb; the believers inviting the deceased to join in the enjoyment by calling out 'Vibas!' (Live!). These were no attempts at resurrection, but a wholly different view of death to that which was found in most of the centuries to come.

But this comfort with death did not mean that they focussed solely on the Messiah's own passing. Interestingly, when they used art to depict Jesus Christ it was not on the cross that they placed him, not at least, until the fifth century. Christians preferred to use symbols that emphasised Jesus' nurture of life; anchors, doves, boats, olive branches, palm trees, bread, fish, vines and grapes – these were the images that reappeared time and time again. Jesus was frequently more good shepherd than sacrificial lamb. With persecution a very real threat, members of the early Church perhaps had little need to remind themselves of the role of suffering within Christianity. They knew that Christ shared their struggles just as they must share in his.

There's another point to be made about the art of the day; Christians had to be careful how openly 'Christian' they were. In order to fool pagan observers it was common for artists to use

c80
Rome's Colosseum completed

138
Hadrian's Wall completed in Britain

166 – 167
Plague in Roman Empire

235 – 284
Civil war in Roman Empire

classical imagery to disguise a central Christian message. So one small sculpture from the early days of the faith shows a muscular, bearded Jonah emerging from the mouth of a decidedly mythical-looking beast; dragon's head, lion's feet, whale's body and serpent's tail. To the unenlightened observer this was some obscure episode from ancient mythology, but to the Christian it pointed straight back to Jonah, as well, perhaps, as to the current threats of Roman rule and persecution.

However, something was changing – even if most were unaware of the gathering clouds. While scholars like Origen and others like Tertullian had devoted themselves to crafting a living theology, by the end of the fourth century there was an air of decline that could be sensed. The catechistic period reduced from three years to at most the Lenten period. The once controversial sharing of the kiss of peace (where the community of believers would have no other option than to put right any issues that had developed between them) reduced in occurrence and the method of giving changed entirely. Where previously those attending Church gatherings would place their offerings near the door as they entered, the process of the offertory procession became increasingly popular. Christianity, the religion of the 'people of the way', was becoming less bound by 'the way' itself. While decades had passed by with believers whispering in corners and meeting in secret, displays of faith were about to become public. The ground was about to shift in ways that previous generations would have struggled to comprehend, and among the tangled threads there would be both good and bad results.

28 – 75
Buddhism enters
Emperor Ming's China

c67
Peter martyred

64
Nero's Rome burns

70
Siege of Jerusalem

Perhaps that's too much too soon, a little over-eager on the pessimism. History moves more slowly than these words describe and these early days were full of reasons to be cheerful. My favourite? It's this reflection on the Lord's Prayer from Cyprian, the North African bishop who gave his life for his faith just two years after Stephen was the first to be martyred for pursuit of Christ:

> We should live as temples of God that it may be plain to all that God dwells in us. It is important that our conduct should not degenerate and become unworthy of the Spirit. Rather let we who have set out to be heavenly and spiritual, entertain only heavenly and spiritual thoughts and behaviour. For the Lord God himself has declared: 'I will glorify those who glorify me; but those that despise me, I shall despise.' The blessed apostle Paul has likewise stated in one of his letters: 'You are not your own. You were bought at a price; therefore, glorify God in your body.'
>
> [In the Lord's Prayer] we go on to say: 'Hallowed be your name.' We are not envisaging that God will be made holy by our prayers: we are asking rather that his holiness should shine in us. Anyway, by whom could God be sanctified since it is God himself who sanctifies? But observe that in Scripture it is also written: 'Be holy because I am holy.' Thus it should be our earnest desire that we, who have been made holy in baptism, should continue to grow in what we have begun to be; and this we pray every day. We certainly need to be made holy daily because every day we sin, and every day we need to have those

c80
Rome's Colosseum completed

166 – 167
Plague in Roman Empire

138
Hadrian's Wall completed in Britain

235 – 284
Civil war in Roman Empire

> sins washed away. In this we are engaged in a process that makes us ever more deeply sanctified.

Was it that wilful choice to live a better life today, accompanied by the open pursuit of divine grace, that set them apart? Could it really be as simple as that?

Chapter Two

313 – 476
Church of the Roman Empire

He was, after all, one of the greatest generals of the day. Born in what is now the Serbian Republic around AD 274, by the time Flavius Valerius Constantinus reached thirty he had already proved himself a brave and dependable soldier. Campaigns against raging barbarians on the Danube in AD 296 and brutal Persians in Syria in AD 297 and again Mesopotamia from AD 298 to AD 299 elevated him to great heights as he served under the persecutor-in-chief, Emperor Diocletian.

Yet while his boss raced towards his 'baptism of blood', Constantine took a different view of the Christians. Or, at least, he remained on speaking terms with their God.

With Diocletian having retreated into retirement and subsequent death, Constantine found himself at something of a crossroads. The year was AD 312 and it was the eve of battle. Yet this was not against the indecipherable *bar-bar-bar* mumblings of the brutes they dubbed barbarians; this was a battle against one of his own, Maxentius. It was the usual story and the usual prize; a fight between two men for ultimate power, each with no intention of sharing.

On the eve of what was to be the deciding battle, Constantine's thoughts were already far away from the place. His victory was assured – after all, hadn't he survived numerous attempts on his life already, including that incident with the lion that just happened to cross his path while he was alone up near the Danube? No, the real question was not whether he would win, but to which god should he look for help? In whose name should he fight? What sort of ruler should he be?

Choosing divine support like he chose armour, Constantine was

312
Constantine becomes
Roman Emperor

325
First Council of Nicea

330
Constantinople founded
on site of Byzantium

c400
Augustinian Rule
formed

shocked when, some time around noon on the day of his battle with Maxentius, he looked to the sky and saw a cross formed in the sun. The words 'Conquer By This' formed in his mind, and the most significant conversion since Saul of Tarsus was in play.

Of course he won the battle and once the power was fully his, Emperor Constantine I worked to protect and promote the faith, involving himself in the politics of Christianity in way never seen before.

Constantine's conversion was the start point of a whole range of positive outcomes. At the beginning of the fourth century, only five per cent of those living under Roman rule were Christians. A hundred years later Christianity was as powerful a force as it has ever been, with estimates putting global membership of the faith at forty per cent.

There was no more need for secrecy. New believers were able to celebrate the lives and deaths of their heroes in public and the practice of pilgrimage became increasingly important and popular. Constantine's own mother, Helena, went to Jerusalem, like so many other Christians in search of a greater connection with a past covered over by centuries of persecution and underground retreats. She returned with artefacts from, and insight into, the backdrop to Christ's life – of varying degrees of authenticity. She returned with the four nails with which Christ was supposedly pinned to the cross (which, incidentally, Helena was convinced had not one but two horizontal cross-pieces). This was to prove controversial for centuries, but not merely because of the claim to possess the actual nails themselves. It was the very number which

410
Sack of Rome

432
St Patrick brings Christianity to Ireland

445
Attila the Hun invades Western Europe

476
Fall of Emperor Romulus Augustulus

would divide people. By claiming that there were four nails, Helena – like most others - believed Christ was crucified with legs slightly apart, one nail in each foot or ankle. By the time the thirteenth century arrived there would be many other who believed that this was wrong, that there were in fact only three nails used; one for each hand or wrist and just one going through both feet or ankles. The division would become yet another difference between Orthodox and Roman Churches. Those who, like Helena, believed in the presence of four nails joined the Orthodox view of the crucifixion, a more subtle, slightly restrained (if crucifixion can ever be said to be so) version when compared to the brutality of the three-nail execution. In time the simple matter of a single nail would be used to stress far greater differences between the wings of the Church, with the east favouring the divinity of God's son while the west looked to his humanity for inspiration.

Back in the early fourth century, however, such divisions were far off. Instead, transformation was the order of the day. Even the very architecture of Rome changed as a result of the Emperor's new faith. Once a sort of town hall/courthouse variant, the *basilica* was handed over to the Christians, its unimpressive exterior masking a lavishly decorated interior. *Martyria* arrived - shrines to martyrs, built in the round like pagan temples but with more gold and flair. The inconspicuous house churches fell out of use, as the anonymous was traded-in for the highly public.

The Emperor's embracing of Christianity altered the sectors of authority within the Church itself, and these new buildings created

312
Constantine becomes Roman Emperor

325
First Council of Nicea

330
Constantinople founded on site of Byzantium

c400
Augustinian Rule formed

new roles. The priest now had far more to do, and with the increasing numbers gathering to attend services it was important to make sure that those who really needed to be close to the action were seated appropriately. Gradually the congregation found themselves punted down one end of the building while the priest and his crew got on with the important stuff up the other. Still, some traditions remained; the Eucharist was performed in the middle of the gathered believers.

Bishops became increasingly important. With more people to oversee, their work began to take on elements of the political, and their new found status was reflected in the fact that they were allowed to use the imperial postal service to communicate with others, just like other members of the ruling elite.

Art became a vital tool for many as they pursued a deeper understanding of God. The numbers coming through the front door simply meant that the laborious, one-to-one method of nurturing faith had to be replaced by a more efficient approach.

With the shackles finally off, Christians found that they were also able to have a say in the way that society treated others. Rome had never rated social conscience much – the Empire had always played things according to a 'survival of the fittest' script, believing in peace through victory, rather than the other way around. Yet Christians were now able to encourage the state towards a more humane and compassionate treatment of others. Where giving to the poor or those who were alien had previously done little to inspire fellow citizens, the Church was now able to champion significant developments like a welfare system and an early form of

410
Sack of Rome

432
St Patrick brings Christianity to Ireland

445
Attila the Hun invades Western Europe

476
Fall of Emperor Romulus Augustulus

legal aid. Bishops were permitted to arbitrate in local disputes, and – practical as ever – many Romans converted to take advantage of the free legal help.

But, of course, there were – and still are – those who consider Constantine's conversion as the precursor to a whole series of negative developments within Christianity. Some even go so far as to declare that Constantine's conversion was the *worst thing that ever happened to the Church*. According to the logic, the Emperor was guilty of taking what was previously a revolutionary, underground insurgency and corrupting it with safety and a lust for power.

Can someone finding faith in Christ ever really be considered a wholly bad thing? Isn't the real problem that Constantine was simply not converted *enough*? Intent on revitalising what was an ailing Roman empire, his magnetic north always seemed to be power rather than grace and truth. In other words, what would have happened if Constantine's conversion had taken him all the way from power-hungry sceptic to devoted servant and disciple of Christ? What if he had abandoned far more of his previous appetites and assumptions and upgraded them instead with the approach that many of those in the early Church had adopted? What if he'd followed Origen's lead, or Cyprian's?

I suppose it's hardly surprising that Constantine imposed his authority upon the Church. Having the boss come and fiddle with the design department was the price for protection. But his interference was not insignificant, and the tinkering did have unhelpful consequences for the Church. The Emperor's behaviour in what

312
Constantine becomes Roman Emperor

325
First Council of Nicea

330
Constantinople founded on site of Byzantium

c400
Augustinian Rule formed

became known as the Arian conflict makes it all perfectly clear.

It all starts with the contentious issue of the relationship between God and Christ. Back in the second century Justin Martyr supported the idea laid out in the Gospel of John of the 'logos' – a term for Jesus that held him as the culmination of all truth and philosophies (as sort of ultimate revelation of all man's previous wonderings and best guesses). Origen carried the idea on, suggesting that within the trinity existed a hierarchy; the Father was greatest, then the Son, then the Spirit.

These ideas had been in flux for decades. Nothing had been decided formally, but then Arius – a priest from Alexandia - showed up. He made a bit of a fuss. According to Arius the Son was not divine. Yes, he was really pretty impressive – rather like an archangel - but to say that he was God simply did not make sense.

For his troubles he was exiled in Palestine where, like all the very best revolutionaries, he wrote protest songs. Eventually Constantine felt that he had to involve himself, so he stepped in and ordered the Church to fix it. And so it was that in 325 a few hundred bishops met at Nicaea to agree that they were right in the first place and that the condemnation of Arius was fair. Together they came up with the Nicene creed, the central expression of faith that sought to clarify once and for all what Christianity was really about;

> We believe in one God, the Father Almighty, Maker of all
> things visible and invisible.
> And in one Lord Jesus Christ, the Son of God, begotten of the

410
Sack of Rome

432
St Patrick brings Christianity to Ireland

445
Attila the Hun invades Western Europe

476
Fall of Emperor Romulus Augustulus

Father [the only-begotten; that is, of the essence of the Father, God of God], Light of Light, very God of very God, begotten, not made, being of one substance with the Father;
by whom all things were made [both in heaven and on earth];
who for us men, and for our salvation, came down and was incarnate and was made man;
he suffered, and the third day he rose again, ascended into heaven
from thence he shall come to judge the quick and the dead.
And in the Holy Ghost.

How does this show Constantine in a bad light? The venue for the meeting was the Emperor's choice, and his reasons were clear; Nicaea's location made it possible for him to keep an eye on the construction of his ambitious project to build a new Rome. This exclusively Christian city – modestly named Constantinople – would have no shrines or temples and, according to the master's intentions, it would become the centre of power for all Christianity. Clearly, Constantine was in need of relearning some of the most basic, fundamental lessons about the very nature of Christianity and the sovereignty of God. But I suppose he was neither the first nor the last political leader who confused earthly power with divine blessing.

While it appears that Constantine was not so heavy handed as others suggest – he was less involved in the main discussion than he could have been – it was in the years that followed that his meddling became a real problem. While the bishops believed that the matter

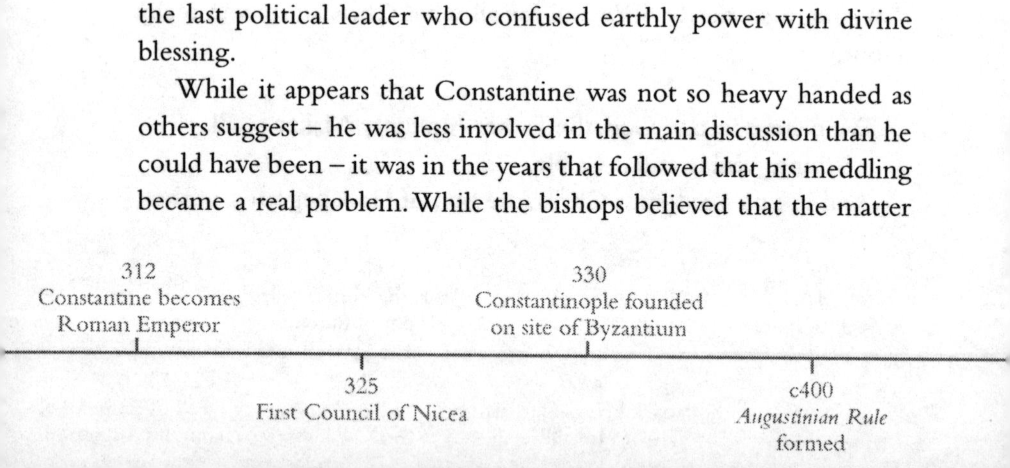

had been put to bed, the tuneful theologian was nowhere near finished; Arius refused to stay silent and continued to criticise Church doctrine.

Eventually – by 336 – Arius had made so much noise that Constantine returned to the issue. In fact, the ruler decided that since so many people were now following Arius's line, the original counsel at Nicaea must have got it wrong. So he ordered the church to reverse the decision. Which it did.

This was a problem. Constantine was now calling himself a bishop; how would the Church deal with the massive ramifications of a politician dictating to the Church?

Fortunately, I suppose, Arius died. In a toilet in Constantinople. Yet the problems remained. Even when Constantine himself died the next year in 337.

Was this the end of the trouble? Could the church now get back to work, enjoying the benefits of its new-found liberty? Not at all.

Constantine's three sons took over the family business. Either through raging ego or lack or imagination, the Emperor painted from a limited pallet when it came to naming his sons, so it was Constantine II who was given the western area of the empire, Constans that received the central portion while Constantinus oversaw the eastern region. Before long three became two when Constantine II was killed by Constans. The Roman Empire was thus divided – not for the first time – into a Latin speaking western half and a Greek speaking eastern half. Yet with two brothers ready to fight and blood already on Constans' hands, it is not hard to predict the outcome.

410
Sack of Rome

432
St Patrick brings Christianity to Ireland

445
Attila the Hun invades Western Europe

476
Fall of Emperor Romulus Augustulus

Arius had built an impressive following, and his simple logic was surely part of the appeal; if God was uncreated, how could something created by God *be* God? Arius had followers – called Arians (although many rejected the name since Arius was only a humble priest) – as well as his opponents who replied that Christ was 'begotten' – a process that did not involve being created.

Constans and the majority of Christians in the west opposed Arius' ideas. Constantinus and the rest of the eastern Christians largely signed up to the Arian view of Christ, and the emperor made use of his power by deposing those who disagreed and encouraging the people of Alexandria to do the same. These eastern dwellers were suspicious of the Latin speaking Christians who saw no difference between Father and Son. Things got serious too – as well as strange – with the likes of the lynching of George the Cappodocian. He was tied to a camel and burned to death.

The death of Constans in 350 (killed, it turned out by assassins working as part of a failed military coup) eventually meant that Constantinus became ruler of the entire Roman empire, east and west. He held councils to attempt to quash anti-Arian pressure and in 355 took a significant step into the history books while bishops were arguing in Milan at one of his councils. Frustrated by the lack of progress, Constantinus emerged from behind the curtain where he had been hiding, forcing the clergy to do his bidding and sign the decree.

Six years later he was dead and the chaos continued. He was succeeded by his cousin Julian who did what he could to de-

312
Constantine becomes
Roman Emperor

330
Constantinople founded
on site of Byzantium

325
First Council of Nicea

c400
Augustinian Rule
formed

Christianise the empire. He called back the worship of pagan Gods and restored previously exiled bishops in the hope that the confusion and discord that followed would suffocate the religion once and for all.

His own death was not long in coming, and after Julian there were yet more brief terms of office, untimely deaths, division and the slow descent of a once great power. Arianism started to lose its appeal and influence, and in 381 the Council of Constantinople ruled that the Spirit was also divine. Arianism was all but gone, yet the Church was still alive. Against all odds it would outlast the Roman empire. Yet at what cost?

THE SEARCH FOR AUTHENTICITY

While the lines between Christianity and political power blurred among the seats of power, Christianity had been spreading from cities to rural areas. There, Anthony – a rich Egyptian – heard the command to 'sell what you have and give it to the poor'. Which he did. The man spent fifteen years living among tombs in pursuit of a life of simplicity. Yet the tombs were too easy, too much of a distraction; the middle of desert called.

And so Anthony – his wealth little more than a vague memory – moved to live among the heat and the dust and the difficulty of the desert. Hidden behind high walls he relied on scraps thrown to him by kind supporters. Such was the dramatic nature of his life that his popularity rose rapidly, attracting many followers. Eventually the hermit gave in to the clamours of the public and a community of simple-living Christians formed near the Red Sea.

410
Sack of Rome

432
St Patrick brings Christianity to Ireland

445
Attila the Hun invades Western Europe

476
Fall of Emperor Romulus Augustulus

This retreat tapped into a sense that time was up for the Roman Empire – or, at least, that Christianity's success was not reliant on the affirmation and protection of those who held political power. It also underlined the sense that a life lived in pursuit of Christ's ideas should leave one with something to say about egregious social problems.

For those in pursuit of a more authentic expression of Christianity like Anthony's followers by the Red Sea, sex was off the agenda. It had been an issue for Christians for some time, even as far back as the second century when Justin proclaimed that 'either we do not marry except to rear children, or we refuse to marry and we exercise complete self-control'. Tertullian was even more specific in explaining why sex should be treated with caution:

> In that very heart of extreme gratification, do we not feel that something of our soul has gone out from us? ... by continence you will buy up a great stock of sanctity, by making savings on the flesh you will be able to invest in the Spirit.

So sex was reserved for reproduction, not pleasure. This denial of sensory stimulation was in contrast to the traditional Jewish beliefs burned deep into the collective memory. Their arrival in a 'land flowing with milk and honey' opened the door to sensory delight and satisfaction of appetites. For the early Church – confronted by lasciviousness and greed – denial appeared to be the only way forward. 'Our desire,' explained one writer at the time 'is not to experience desire at all.' Even laughter was frowned upon. The

312
Constantine becomes Roman Emperor

325
First Council of Nicea

330
Constantinople founded on site of Byzantium

c400
Augustinian Rule formed

gap between Christianity and Judaism widened further still.

In the West the clergy took this to heart. At the start of the fourth century the Council of Elvira in southern Spain claimed that bishops should abstain from sex, while in the east it was not so. Their cousins in the east, on the other hand, were allowed to marry, have sex and – presumably – a whole lot more fun.

Of course, when sex made its way into the sermon, the question of Mary's virginity could not be far behind. It was increasingly contentious, and by the second century she was widely considered to be a perpetual virgin. Young women followed her perceived example, as did widows, regaining through chastity their virginity and protecting the Church as a result.

The sense of retreat continued in Egypt, Syria and Palestine. Each territory was host to hermits. In the 320s an ex-soldier from Constantine's army wrote a set of rules for his own self-supporting community – with individuals pooling both their physical resources and their money. Pachomius had hit on something, and even though the emphasis was less on prayer and meditation, the early stages of the monastic movement were underway. By the time he died in 346 there were eleven communities, more than enough to establish those in pursuit of being alone (Greek = *monachos*) as the earliest monks.

Some of these communities pushed the self-denial aspect more than others. In Nitria (south of Alexandria) in 300 more than 5,000 monks lived in isolation from the rest of the growing Church. Each monk had their own one or two-roomed cell which they would personally have built in a day or so with the help of others. These cells might have been miles away from the central church where the main meetings were held and where meals of bread, olive oil, lentils, fish and wine were shared. The collective aim was to reduce rather than increase human desire for material things, in the process making the body holy by regulating both sleep and food. As they became at ease with life they hoped to be able to better focus on and find God.

In searching for evidence of their character, one text from the time stands out even today;

> An old man was asked , 'How can I find God?' He replied, 'In fasting, in watching, in labours, in devotion, and above all, in discernment. I tell you, many people have injured their bodies without discernment and have gone away from us having achieved nothing. Our mouths smell bad through fasting, we know the Scriptures by heart, we can recite all the Psalms of David, but we do not have that which God seeks: charity and humility.
>
> Benedicta Ward, *The Wisdom of the Desert Fathers*, 90, p.29

AUGUSTINE OF HIPPO

Born in 354, Augustine was not a monk, yet he felt the pull towards them. Often known as the father of the western Church, Augustine was something of a late starter. It was not until he was thirty-two that a moment of tranquillity was transformed into a pivotal point after which his life would never quite be the same. Alone in a garden, Augustine felt sure that he heard a child's voice say 'Pick up and read'.

312
Constantine becomes Roman Emperor

325
First Council of Nicea

330
Constantinople founded on site of Byzantium

c400
Augustinian Rule formed

Reaching for the scriptures he turned at random to Paul's letter to Romans: 'Put on the Lord Jesus Christ and make no provision for the flesh, to satisfy its desires.'

That was all the invitation he needed to adopt communal life. Interestingly enough, Augustine was unable ever to become a monk, yet throughout his life he pursued his faith with a discipline that inspired countless followers. Bishop, writer, teacher, preacher, Augustine understood the goodness of creation and fought for the unity and future perfection of Church. His mind travelled widely grasping with the necessity of grace instead of the overblown self-importance of self-perfection, perceiving evil as the absence of good and sin as the abuse of free will.

Today his work remains as potent as it is relevant;

> In one of the Psalms it is written, 'You, O Lord, are the same and your years will never end.' My brothers and sisters, do our years never end? They slip away from us day by day. Those years which have been no longer exist; those which lie in the future have yet to be given us. What is past is dead, and what is to come will likewise, in due course, pass into oblivion. Today, my friends, this moment in which we speak, is all that exists. The first hours of today have already passed, the remainder of the day has yet to come; come it will, but only to pass into oblivion … Nothing that exists remains constant. Even the human body is subject to a continual process of change; it has no permanence. It ages, it changes with the passage of time and the circumstances of our lives, with

disease and accident. It has no constancy. Even the stars have no constancy: they go through patterns of their own, though these changes are not always obvious to us. They move in relation to one another, they whirl through space, moving from east to west, and back again towards the east. They do not rest; they are not the same.

Nor is the human heart any more constant! Consider how many thoughts and distractions assail it. Consider the effect pleasure has upon us, how various cravings wreak havoc inside us. The human mind is termed rational, but it too changes and possesses no stability. One moment we want something; the next we change our mind. One moment we are convinced of something; the next we are no longer so sure. One moment we remember; the next moment we forget. No one has an inner coherence of being… it is really important to allow all this frustration, these diseases, these difficulties, troubles and pains, to humble us so that we return to the One who is always the same. And let us enter that city whose inhabitants share the stability [of God].

Exposition of Psalm 121

It could have been written just for today. With all our speed and shifts and unreliable changes going off at the speed of sound, the words of Augustine could be an anchor for our souls. They could keep us in check, hold us down in the storms and prevent age old mistakes from being made.

That's what he was doing back then; gradually, Augustine was

312
Constantine becomes
Roman Emperor

330
Constantinople founded
on site of Byzantium

325
First Council of Nicea

c400
Augustinian Rule
formed

writing a new map for the journey of the Church. His plans took the believers off in a slightly different direction, rejecting the gluttony of those seduced by power and bringing back to the city the revolutionary nature of those whose lives were dependent on God alone.

Others who were in pursuit of divine revelation through monastic discipline included the Cappadocian Fathers, remembered even today as significant theologians of the fourth century. As part of a monastic family, and led by their sister, Abbess Makrina, the three brothers studied and meditated with significant results. They proved that Christians did not need to hide their faith – or their knowledge – from educated Greek-speaking intellectuals. While it was true that Christianity was at odds with much of the work of Plato, Aristotle and other Greek Philosophers, the teachings of Jesus had led scholars like the Cappadocian Fathers to develop an understanding of the nature of humanity that could go head to head with the ancient greats. The brothers thought, talked and taught in great depth about the Trinity and at the First Council of Constantinople in 381 saw their influence come to bear on the final version of the Nicene Creed, adding, in particular, the following;

> And in the Holy Ghost, the Lord and Giver of life, who proceedeth from the Father, who with the Father and the Son together is worshiped and glorified, who spake by the prophets. In one holy catholic and apostolic Church; we acknowledge one baptism for the remission of sins; we look for the resurrection of the dead, and the life of the world to come. Amen.

410
Sack of Rome

432
St Patrick brings Christianity to Ireland

445
Attila the Hun invades Western Europe

476
Fall of Emperor Romulus Augustulus

THE CRACKS IN THE WALLS

But the story was not as simple as that. Discord and disagreement were the common rhythms of the Church by now, and it wasn't unusual for groups to split off from previous bodies and follow a new bishop. The Novatians tried it and managed to establish themselves as true opponents of the Rome-based Church, but eventually they failed and disappeared from active memory.

Another schism went to the heart of the matter that troubled many in the fourth century: what should be done about those 'Christians' who had caved under pressure from Roman persecution? The wider Church was happy to allow them back in, yet many saw this as compromise. With its roots in the Diocletian persecution, the Donatists became an immensely popular Church that railed against such traitors (originally known as 'traditors' from the word describing the way they handed over their Scriptures for burning by the agents of Emperor Diocletian's persecution.

These Donatists strove for religious purity, but elements of their membership were pretty handy in a fight. They mastered guerrilla warfare with their militant members becoming known as Circumcelliones, carrying clubs called 'israels', attacking Catholic churches, and hoping for a taste of martyrdom themselves.

While the thugs strutted and struck out, the eastward-spreading Byzantine Churches still debated the nature of Christ; was he divine or human? Another council meeting at Chalcedon (influenced again

312
Constantine becomes
Roman Emperor

330
Constantinople founded
on site of Byzantium

325
First Council of Nicea

c400
Augustinian Rule
formed

by the Trinitarian teaching of the Cappadocian Fathers) attempted to soothe fraying tempers, but many in the east resented the west's dabbling, and were subsequently left with a new focus for their frustration.

Meanwhile, a fiery-tempered preacher named Pelagius was taking matters into his own hands, opposing the lack of integrity that was infecting the Church by upping the moral rhetoric and re-marking the hard line. Individuals were responsible for their own behaviour and God's rules were set out for a purpose; our obedience. Augustine, however, had other ideas. For him God's grace was a defining influence. Our inherited failings and sinful nature could only be fixed through God alone, and the list of those to be saved is authored by God alone. The conflict between predestination and redemption through human effort, of grace versus works, failed to die down despite the fact that Augustine came out with significantly more support than Pelagius. In their way, both would be proved right at different times ahead, and their clash would repeat throughout the centuries to come.

But enough of the future, there were problems enough back then in the present to concern people. How could the Church continue to exist like this? Yes, it was spread across thousands of miles, with different cultures and traditions all covered beneath its wings, but for many it was vital that the discord only go so far. Augustine and others urged all those who would listen to work to make the church one single, whole entity. They criticised the Donatists for doing precisely the opposite but there was air of inevitability about their efforts.

410
Sack of Rome

432
St Patrick brings Christianity to Ireland

445
Attila the Hun invades Western Europe

476
Fall of Emperor Romulus Augustulus

In 410 Rome was sacked by the Visigoths and the barbarian army. After almost half a millennium, the world as many knew it was over. The Barbarians were allowed to settle … but the Huns were to follow. Christian culture was under threat.

Chapter Three

476 – 699
The Early Middle Ages

There is a basket and there is some rope. We are above a squat city wall against which the empty basket and rope lie, and we are looking down, wondering, perhaps, what on earth is going on. Then it happens; a nervous-looking man edges along the top of the wall and – helped by another – climbs into the basket and is lowered down to the dusty scrub beneath.

This is not Damascus and the man dangling towards escape has no past misted by persecution. It is Rome, 590, and the whispers in the shadows tell you that the Pope has just died. Our man in the basket has nothing to do with his death, but everything to do with what happens next. Like Paul, he carries the potential to transform the future fortunes of the Church – to bring change, life and growth where it is desperately needed. He will lead the Church into a period of renewed integrity and much needed growth. This tangled, fearful, slowly descending man is Gregory, Abbot of St Andrew's. He also happens to be the next Pope.

The only problem is this; he wants absolutely nothing to do with the job at all.

A SIDELINE: WHY POPE?

Literally meaning 'father', in the early days of Christianity the term *Papa* was bestowed on any number of Church leaders or bishops. While he was not known by the title at the time, Saint Peter is still held by many to be the first true Pope. Presiding over the Church of Rome for a quarter century until AD 67 (when he was martyred by Nero) Peter was appointed by Jesus as the first of the apostles and head of his Church – the rock on which it would be built.

[illegible] ...halcedon

590
Gregory I becomes Pope

529
Monte Cassino, Benedictine monastery, founded

597
Augustine's mission to Britain

Protestant scholars perhaps view Peter differently. They suggest that at the time the Bishop of Rome held no more real power than, for example, the Bishop of Antioch or Jerusalem. Either way, by the time Constantine lent his support to the faith it was clear that since Rome was indeed the hub of Christianity, the city's bishop held significantly more influence than the others. Along with the established spiritual authority came an increasingly significant temporal power. The title of Pope was set and the spiritual oversight of the entire Church laid placed in his care. By the time our friend in the basket is attempting to escape, significant oversight is precisely what is needed.

Why? Because the Church is not in a good state. In fact, it's in a terrible condition. Despite the rise of those in dedicated pursuit of simplicity and integrity, the politics of power have infected and weakened many of those in authority.

The status of Mary, mother of Jesus, remains a highly contentious issue. Precisely *what* was she? Was the Greek term *theotokos* (literally translated as *God-bearer* or *the one who gives birth to God*) more divisive than it was helpful? Was it right to consider her as more than a mere physical vessel or did those that elevated her above the status of the rest of mere humanity contradict the essence of Scripture? Besides, since Christians had been used to praying at the gravesides of fallen friends, why shouldn't they ask Mary to intervene for them? If she was chosen for so vital a task, surely her interventions from beyond the grave would carry significant weight?

These conversations and arguments about Mary were also disagreements about Jesus himself. Just as he shared her blood it was

c600
Height of Maya civilization, Central America

610 – 632
Text of Koran revealed to Mohammed

618
Tang dynasty begins, China

636
Jerusalem falls to Muslim armies

logical to ask whether she shared in any of his divinity. And while Arius had argued, strummed and sang with great success in the fourth century, by the time the fifth century came around the Arian crisis began to look like a storm in a teacup by comparison. Where Arius had questioned the nature of the Trinity, Christians now debated the person of Christ himself; how did the part of him that was human relate to the fully divine Trinity?

Perhaps the only factor that deflected some of the heat about this new Christological controversy was its location. Arianism had been debated across the entire Roman Empire, east and west. These days, however, the Roman Empire had been trimmed down somewhat into its new Byzantine version, confined to the eastern Mediterranean and Middle East. While northern Europe previously only offered mumbling barbarian hoards, the Franks had emerged to threaten and push back Rome's previous advances.

So this was a controversy that was held in the east, and started out as a battle between the two most powerful leaders in the Church of this Byzantine era. On the one side was Cyril, Alexandria's pre-eminent leader. In the blue corner was Nestorius, the big man on campus in Constantinople.

The people of Alexandria had always been a tad iffy about the Constantinople types. After all, Alexandria had history on its side – almost six hundred years by this point – while Constantinople was a suckling infant conceived in the lusty self-interest of Constantine's ego. They were never going to get along, and when Nestorius started to propose that Jesus' nature was a composite of both God the Son and Jesus the human being, Cyril hit back with accusations that

451
Council of Chalcedon

529
Monte Cassino, Benedictine monastery, founded

590
Gregory I becomes Pope

597
Augustine's mission to Britain

Nestorius believed in two Christs rather than the orthodox one.

Cyril's viewpoint went further – it carried on after his death in 444, eventually developing into the concept that Jesus' single nature was in fact purely divine, the human bit having been absorbed by that which was God. And while it might have only taken me a single sentence to outline it here, the controversy was – and is today – one of the major fault lines upon which the Church is laid. Of course every generation and every current learns to appreciate the taste of being right; we all like to believe we have a better understanding of the nature of Jesus. I'm beginning to wonder quite how original – or how right – we ever really can be.

Anyway, back with Cyril and Nestorius. Attempts to sort things out in grand meetings failed to have the desired effect. In Ephesus a council in 431 found that Cyril was on the right track and condemned Nestorius. Twenty years later and the issue remained live and unresolved. Leo, bishop of Rome intervened, criticising the evolution of Cyril's ideas and attempting to find a middle ground between the two leaders. A further council in 451 at Chalcedon, near Constantinople, reiterated once again the criticism of those who had taken the argument to its extremes. Some accepted its rulings and became the orthodox majority in Byzantium. Pope Leo's attempts to offer a third way also proved popular among believers over in the west, but to many in the eastern Church it was little more than a tepid and unwelcome intrusion. Finally, Chalcedon's bishops ruled that the authority of the Church in Constantinople – New Rome – was equal in authority to that of the elder Rome.

With the Church already divided into Arians, Montanists (who

c600
Height of Maya civilization, Central America

618
Tang dynasty begins, China

610 – 632
Text of Koran revealed to Mohammed

636
Jerusalem falls to Muslim armies

some say emerged centuries later in the form of Pentecostals), Donatists and similarly grace-less Novatians, now came Nestorians, Chalcedonians and Monophysites ('one-naturites'). Geography played a part in the divisions too, with Europe largely receptive to those still following Arius, Egypt and Syria accepting the Monophysite view of things while Nestorian theology headed into Persia and beyond.

So much for the unified Church.

***

The Church was sick. Not only was it divided and battle scarred from internal struggles, it was also stained by corruption. The Council at Chalcedon attempted to address some of these behavioural issues, as well as the larger theological problems. From the sale of positions within the Church to the forming of violent mobs by clergy, evidence of the Church's slipping moral standards was clear and desperately needed to be addressed.

Our friend in the basket was the Church's best hope of redemption. Pope Gregory I would eventually be known as the Doctor of the Church, a one-man restoration of a body sapped of so much strength and authority.

Gregory was born into wealth yet experienced at first hand the turmoil of life in a city under siege. Rome was overtaken three times during his youth and when, by the time he was thirty, Gregory was appointed Prefect of the City it might have appeared that he was already taking steps on a familiar path towards political greatness. Yet

451 Council of Chalcedon

529 Monte Cassino, Benedictine monastery, founded

590 Gregory I becomes Pope

597 Augustine's mission to Britain

Gregory shunned the position and the prospects and became a monk instead, giving away his personal fortune to establish seven monasteries.

After only three years of simplicity and seclusion, Gregory was once again elevated to higher office. The pope needed him in the court of Byzantium, and for six years he struggled to hold true to his monastic values in the face of Byzantine courtly extravagant excess.

Once back at his favoured St Andrew's a chance encounter with blond-haired English boys – not 'Angles' as Gregory was told, but 'Angels' as he called them – set up a potential mission trip to England. Gregory, however, was obedient when the recall came from Rome after only three days travel north. Yet later, once Pope Pelagius II had died and Gregory the Great was in office, he would send Augustine (not the one who preached grace and brawled with the theology of Pelagius – that was a different Augustine) up to convert the Anglo-Saxons of England and establish a successful Church among them. That in turn would send missionaries out to Germany and the Netherlands, cementing the restoration of the Church in the west – something that had largely slipped from view in the decades before. And as Rome's power became gradually shared with Germanic tribes, Christians began to proselytise beyond the confines of the Roman Empire.

Gregory's problems were not limited to a declining western Church. Italy was in crisis as floods ruined crops and grain stores and in 589, Rome itself was rocked by disease and the streets emptied of people – apart from those transporting corpses out to mass graves beyond the city walls. Perhaps these memories were what slowed him

c600
Height of Maya civilization, Central America

618
Tang dynasty begins, China

610 – 632
Text of Koran revealed to Mohammed

636
Jerusalem falls to Muslim armies

as he tried to escape in the basket once Pope Pelagius II died in February 590.

His final fourteen years were spent working at a frantic pace. Perhaps he was hoping to work himself out of a job, to be able to return to the monastic solitude he craved. It seems that his body was in revolt, plaguing him with cramps, fevers and gout.

Never one to use the title 'Pope' himself, Gregory urged the Church to consider personal integrity a priority. Public penance and displays of religious ritual were held up to the light, and Gregory was at pains to emphasise the importance of private penance. By caring for the city's many refugees he restored some of the early Church's sense of social responsibility and by referring to himself as 'servant of the servants of the Lord' he reversed the traditional Pope's pursuit of world domination and replaced it with humility and sacrifice.

Back on track? Perhaps. The splits remained and the rot would take more than fourteen years to treat fully, but with a renewed sense of optimism, an expanding Church and a refreshed awareness of the links between lifestyle and faith, Christianity emerged into the Middle Ages in far better shape.

It needed to be, for it was about to face one of its greatest ever challenges.

ISLAM'S BIRTH

It was a battle at first. It might not have appeared as such – Muhammad ibn Abdullah sitting alone in the caves a few miles out of town from his birthplace, Mecca – but it was a battle all right.

Spending months in prayer and meditation, Muhammad reflected

451
Council of Chalcedon

529
Monte Cassino, Benedictine monastery, founded

590
Gregory I becomes Pope

597
Augustine's mission to Britain

on the paganism that ruled his home town. In 610, aged forty, Muhammad's prayers were interrupted one morning by a voice he took to be of the angel Gabriel. He was delivering the word of God, and dictated the text of the Koran.

Emerging from the cave Muhammad's preached against the polytheism, drunkenness and impurity that had overtaken his community. For twelve years the message grew louder and supporters more numerous until, in 622, Muhammad and his followers were forced to leave Mecca, settling instead in Medina.

The similarities between Islam, Christianity and Judaism in those days were clear; the Scriptures were revered, God praised and the shared ancestry from Abraham celebrated. But according to Islam the Trinity was too lax for their strict monotheistic tastes, and the divinity of Jesus was out of the question. Still, according to Muhammad, Jews and Christians were *Dhimmi* – 'people under custody or protection' – and their presence could be tolerated, more or less.

Tolerated for a time. Eventually, after Muhammad's death in 632, the freshly unified Arabian peninsula was ready to flex its muscles. Under the leadership of Muhammad's father in law Egypt, Armenia and then Persia were attacked and conquered. In 635 the Byzantine army was dispatched to deal with the insurgents, yet they were engulfed and wiped out by a sandstorm. By the time three years had passed, both Jerusalem and Damascus had fallen beneath Islam's sword.

In the same year Christianity was officially recognised in China and the Celts who were spread across northern Europe were adapting to life in service of Christ. Never particularly keen on their imperial

c600
Height of Maya civilization, Central America

610 – 632
Text of Koran revealed to Mohammed

618
Tang dynasty begins, China

636
Jerusalem falls to Muslim armies

neighbours, the Celts developed certain flavours in their expression of Christian faith, and the different approach taken to, for example, the English led to conflict. Eventually the English won and Britain declared its spiritual allegiance to the Church of Rome.

Yet still the Muslims kept on coming. Barely a few years since they came into existence, their growth was phenomenal, sweeping out the old corruption with a new, improved formula. Lifestyle was regulated and theology simplified. For too long the Church had drifted into dangerous territory, its taste for self-interest and greed leaving it vulnerable and weak. Could it ever regain its strength?

Chapter Four

700 – 1499

Too Much Time

Charles the Great
Six words is all it takes:
'By the sword and the cross'.

Charles the Great, Charlemagne, King of the Franks and Emperor of the Holy Roman Empire: those six words in the sentence above this paragraph are all that is needed to bottle up the essence of his rule.

By the time he was 26 Charles - along with his younger brother who died a few years later - had inherited the kingdom of the Christianised-Franks from his father; lands that spread from modern-day Denmark in the north, across France, Germany, Austria and beyond. Hit by two deaths in a handful of years Charles had little room for grieving. The kingdom was in a mess; the Franks were slipping back towards barbarian habits, ditching education and religion in favour of other, less noble pursuits. Up in the northern parts of Europe the Saxons were raging like the true pagans they were, while further south the Roman Catholic Church was battered and suppressed by the victorious invasion of the Lombards. Europe was in chaos and it would take someone with incredible power to fix it.

Charlemagne felt that he was the man for the job. For thirty years his military campaign edged him closer to his objective, and by the time of his death in 814 his empire encompassed most of Western Europe – 9 million square miles in total.

A man of faith (as well as multiple mistresses), Charlemagne's sword and cross were used together; many, like the Saxons, were given the simple choice of converting to Christianity or facing death.

800
Charlemagne becomes Emperor

1096 – 1270
The Crusades

1173
Saladin becomes Sultan of Egypt

1206
Genghis Khan founds Mongol Empire

Unsurprisingly the numbers of the faithful grew dramatically, and the combination of Charlemagne's allegiance to the Church of Rome and his ever-expanding kingdom reflected much of the unity and power of the old Roman Empire.

Others noticed this too. On Christmas Day in 800, while Charlemagne knelt in prayer in Saint Peter's in Rome, Pope Leo III reportedly burst in and surprised the king by placing a golden crown on his bowed head, declaring him emperor and heir to Rome's great Caesars.

The event is clouded by history. Some say that Charlemagne was frustrated by the Pope's actions, and that he would not have entered the Church had he known the pope's plan. The fact that he never used the new title bears this out, yet others suggest that the Pope would not have dared to act without Charlemagne's knowledge. Whatever the truth it's a reasonable guess that each leader may have held different ideas about who was in authority over whom. Did Charlemagne's vast empire make him supreme over the Church or did Leo's spiritual heavyweight overwhelm the northern king? I suppose these questions were nothing new – after all, hadn't Constantine introduced them back in the fourth century? Perhaps real questions need to be asked not just about whether tension between Church and state exists, but about whether they both emerge intact.

Having said that, a little later on in this chapter we shall see how at times the Church really needed no external help at all when it came to sinking to new levels.

1215
Magna Carta

c1300
Easter Island statues built

1337 – 1453
The Hundred Years' War

c1348
Black Death reaches Europe

WHAT'S SO GREAT ABOUT ICONS?

It was around this time that an old controversy found its way to the surface once again. Another Leo – Emperor, rather than Pope – was under siege. The early momentum of the Muslim army had focussed its attention on Constantinople, and Emperor Leo III had shown considerable tactical acumen to fend them off.

While he might have been a decent enough military commander, when it came to common sense Leo was a little lacking. Since the Muslims seemed in general to be so good at defeating Christians, Leo concluded that their success was built on the fact that the Qur'an prohibited all representational art. In other words, they were winning because they had no icons.

He was not totally alone in his thoughts. Christian communities in Persia had already been forced to destroy all their icons and the images themselves had long been subject of various controversies. For some they were a dangerous portal to a heretical view of Christianity. The most famous of all icons – the Hodegetria (depicting Mary with the infant Christ, and reportedly painted by Saint Luke the Evangelist) – was destroyed by the invading Turks when they sacked Constantinople in 1453. It was credited with healing the sick and the lame, and even saving Constantinople numerous times from invasion. Icons became items to be venerated, and copies were believed to hold just as much power as the original. They even ended up as part of the brewing process when good beer was sought: an icon would be dipped into the barrel in the hope that it would improve the end result. Others in time would wave them at

800
Charlemagne becomes
Emperor

1173
Saladin becomes
Sultan of Egypt

1096 – 1270
The Crusades

1206
Genghis Khan founds
Mongol Empire

fires, bombs and invading troops in the belief that the mere presence of the icon would turn trouble around to return from whence it came.

For those of a less cynical persuasion, icons liberated and democratised the faith. They wrestled power away from the Church, allowing individuals to have in their own home an object of real religious significance. An icon could spread the practice of Christianity in ways that Churches might struggle to do, and the choice of Mary as one of the leading subjects created a more accessible path to God. By connecting with the concept of maternal love and sacrifice, many Christians found Mary to be a vital stepping stone in their own comprehension of God's essential character. In other words, they broke down barriers erected by those who were intent on controlling Christianity. Icons brought back to the people the sense of a direct, personal connection with God – a condition which for some had been in short supply for far too long. They democratised, inspired and educated all in one stroke. They looked pretty nice, too.

At different times throughout the history of Christianity icons have seen their popularity soar and crash. Even today there are Christians measured by the million for whom it might seem abhorrent to even contemplate the destruction of so precious a tool of worship. Then again, the other camp – though smaller – is equally vociferous in its damnation of icons, ranking them only marginally higher than Ouija Boards in The List of Things the True Christian Avoids. It appears as though we've done with the beer-dunking, and while there are still those who go a little overboard

1215
Magna Carta

1337 – 1453
The Hundred Years' War

c1300
Easter Island statues built

c1348
Black Death
reaches Europe

on the veneration of the artefacts, as well as those who periodically trash the things (verbally if not physically), by and large things are a lot more stable.

In 724 the Church caught Leo's anti-icon bug and a couple of bishops from the east expressed their discomfort at the way in which certain believers revered these images. Surely it was getting in the way of true worship of God? And wasn't there something in the Ten Commandments about not worshipping false idols? For the next decade or so the process of icon smashing – iconoclasm – continued until Leo lost interest and moved onto some other issue.

Leo's son – Constantine V – was less easily distracted. He waged war on icons and those who didn't share his leanings towards Monophysitism – the old belief that Christ's humanity and divinity are merged into one single 'nature'. Icons were just far too human for his tastes, and to prove it he called a council together near Chalcedon in 754, stuffed with bishops who agreed with him. Those in opposition were condemned.

Over the following years Constantine V brought a familiar theme back to his rule; persecution. Monks and their monasteries were his target. He raided the buildings and forced the monks to marry. Mobs beat and occasionally killed those that irked them most, and public humiliation was the order of the day.

Constantine's death in 775 marked the end of the persecution, and within a few years the monasteries were filling up once more. Yet the icons themselves continued to emerge as points of contention from time to time over the coming centuries.

800
Charlemagne becomes Emperor

1096 – 1270
The Crusades

1173
Saladin becomes Sultan of Egypt

1206
Genghis Khan founds Mongol Empire

THE STENCH

It wasn't merely Constantine V who had the monopoly on idiocy and cruelty. In 897 Pope Stephen VI wrote himself into books like this with an act of such mindless horror that has rarely been surpassed.

The problem started with his predecessor, Pope Formosus. As bishop of Porto he opposed Pope John VIII, was excommunicated and swore never to return to Rome or to reassume his priestly functions. Still, Pope Marinus followed on from John VIII, absolved Formosus and restored him to his former position. Pope Stephen V came next, and when he died in 891 Formosus was chosen as Pope.

Rome was in trouble. Powerful forces were threatening it from beyond and within its walls, and eventually the powerful princes of Spoleto broke through and forced the Pope to consecrate as emperor one of their own. A year later, opposition rose against the Spoleto shoo-in, and Formosus switched allegiance to Arnulf who he saw as Rome's liberator. Unfortunately the Pope was a little premature, and before he could remove the Spoleto prince Arnulf was forced to retreat to Germany due to ill health. Overwhelmed with sorrow, Formosus died on 4th April 896.

The troubles continued after his death, and he was accused of being a traitor. Yet accusations and posthumous proclamations were not enough. In 897 his successor, Pope Stephen VI, dug up his grave and exhumed the rotting corpse of Formosus. What was left of his body was put on trial, condemned, and defiled. Has any pope ever stooped so low? Well, yes, sadly there have been many. From Holocaust deniers to paedophile priests, murderers to adulterous vagabonds, the Papal office has been occupied by some unsavoury characters over the years. Then again, while they might not have reached the dramatic heights of Stephen VI's role play with the rotting Formosus, every denomination in time has given birth to its own horror stories.

Pope Theodore II restored Formosus' corpse to a Christian burial, and at a council presided over by John IX, the pontificate of Formosus was declared valid and all his acts confirmed. Yet the episode remains one of the clearest indications of how power and greed can corrupt even the loftiest of offices.

CLUNY AND BEYOND

It wasn't all bad. In fact, elements of the history of Christianity are at their very best during this time. Much as the Desert Fathers had understood the need to remove themselves from the city, so too, in 910, did a group of monks in modern day France. A duke paid for the building of a new monastery in Cluny, a little north of Lyon. As the community grew, spirituality and labour became important disciplines, and personal integrity was a premium. Things might have been deteriorating in other parts of the Christian community, yet the Cluny model proved to be a successful one. Within less than a couple of centuries Cluny was not only the largest church in the world and the original blueprint for countless monasteries around the world; it was also the second centre of Christianity in the west after Rome. Right up until the raging secularism of the French Revolution,

800
Charlemagne becomes
Emperor

1096 – 1270
The Crusades

1173
Saladin becomes
Sultan of Egypt

1206
Genghis Khan founds
Mongol Empire

Cluny's walls stood firm, reminding all of the power of the Church uncorrupted.

For some, though, Cluny's return to the ideals of Christ did not go deep enough. Simplicity and integrity were increasingly claimed by those outside the monasteries. Why should holiness be restricted to those who had signed up to Cluny's strict code? Couldn't others find their own way of following Christ's lead? Was all this simplicity and enlightenment only for the monks? And so the spiritual thermostat in Western Europe was turned up. Not only were itinerant preachers welcomed, but other monasteries – like the Carthusians – arrived, with numerous monks taking vows of silence and devoting themselves to a life of hardship, endurance and dedication to God.

Alongside this new wave came the teaching of Anselm, Archbishop of Canterbury – a job which grew to become an almost papal equivalent in years to come. A keen mind allowed him to be one of the first to construct a workable theology that answered key questions about the existence of God. His main tool? Pure logic. Anselm put aside the notion that revelation of God was vital to comprehending the Almighty, Instead he chose to prove the existence of God through a series of logical steps, mainly centred on the exploration of what the very name 'God' might signify. He moved on to apply his reasoning to the question of why Christ died, tackling in his book 'Why God Became Man' the contemporary notion that it was to win us back from the Devil. Instead he argued that since Satan could never own us, Christ's sacrifice was atonement for the grief caused to God by our sinful nature. His beliefs brought him

1215
Magna Carta

1337 – 1453
The Hundred Years' War

c1300
Easter Island statues built

c1348
Black Death
reaches Europe

into conflict with several kings and, like Gregory I, Anselm was later granted the title Doctor of the Church.

Anselm's death at the start of the twelfth century occurred more than one hundred years before the birth of his heir as one of the fathers of Christian theology; Thomas Aquinas. Like Anselm, Aquinas (1225–74) was an intellectual, embracing philosophy as well as theology.

There's a story about Aquinas that pretty much tells us all we need to know. On hearing that their son intended to become a monk, Mr and Mrs Aquinas – or Count Landulf and Theodora Countess of Theate as they were known – were pleased; at last their son had chosen a career that would guarantee influence, power and respectability. However, the young man had other ideas, joined up with the Dominicans and explored the true meaning of the *less is more* maxim. Unimpressed by the poverty their son had heaped upon himself, Aquinas's parents had him seized and held captive at their castle of Monte San Giovanni Campano, a few hours travel southeast of Rome. For a year they held him, even sending in a prostitute in order to tempt him over to the life as a member of the religious elite. Yet Aquinas remained uninterested and unimpressed by their plans. He had an essay to write.

Adopting and adapting the work of philosophical giants Plato and Aristotle, Aquinas opened the eyes of those in, and outside of, the Church. The goal of all human existence was, according to Aquinas, relationship with God. The pursuit of this will impact and reorder our priorities; charity, peace and holiness will all gain in importance. This,

800
Charlemagne becomes
Emperor

1096 – 1270
The Crusades

1173
Saladin becomes
Sultan of Egypt

1206
Genghis Khan founds
Mongol Empire

he felt, was the clearest route to happiness there was.

A little earlier, and a little further south, a young man followed a well-worn path. His father was a wealthy merchant, and while his mother had ideas about him becoming a man of God, Francesco di Bernardone followed the family's male genes. He became a troubadour – a performance poet by any other name – and lived according to the fashion. Yet he was not quite like any other rich kid with a skill for entertaining the crowd. He had a little something extra – compassion. There's a story about him lavishing everything he had in his pockets upon a beggar one day, only to meet with the extreme displeasure of his father.

What we do know is that for a year he was in prison – held captive after being on the losing side in a local battle – and when he returned to Assisi, Francis was beginning to turn his back on the lavish, light-hearted ways that had occupied his time before. Gradually he gave in to the pull that poverty was beginning to have upon his life. Helping lepers, begging on behalf of the poor and eventually – in the church of San Damiano – encountering a mystical vision in which Christ animated through an icon instructed him to 'repair my house'.

Francis of Assisi set to work restoring churches and chapels that had fallen into ruin. Relations with his father deteriorated to the extent that the son renounced him entirely, even stripping off the clothes he had been given. From then on Francis was a beggar around his home region. In time he turned to preaching, wandering the hills of Umbria with a group of companions, singing, serving and finally building an 'order'; a group of like-minded men similarly committed to a life of

1215
Magna Carta

1337 – 1453
The Hundred Years' War

c1300
Easter Island statues built

c1348
Black Death
reaches Europe

simplicity and dedication. And so the Franciscan Monks were born.

A later attempt to bring peace to the Holy Land came close – but not quite close enough – to success. Francis challenged the Sultan to a fire walk, on the condition that the Monk enter first, and if he were to emerge unscathed the Sultan should convert to faith in Christ. The host was not so keen on the idea, yet for years following the end of the Crusader Kingdom, Franciscan monks received a far warmer welcome in the region than others.

The story continued, with tales of stigmata and further mystical encounters set alongside true sacrifice and devotion. Little wonder that two years after his death he was pronounced a saint.

THE SPLIT

While Aquinas may have seen one unified pursuit and Francis of Assisi perceived the importance of simplicity, conformity was not catching. In fact, it's surprising that the Church lasted for so long as one body. The Church that spanned the east and the west, the old Rome of Italy and the New Rome in Constantinople were perhaps always on course to separate. Their many collisions and disagreements simply placing too much strain on bonds that were far too weak to cope.

Eventually, the camel's back gave in to the smallest of straws – or, at least, just one little word: *filioque*. The Nicene Creed had been the key attempt to celebrate common ground between the emerging wings of the Church, yet those in the west felt that it was in need of a little polishing. The line about the Holy Spirit 'who proceeds from the father' was too vague and gave a little too much equal standing for the third person of the Trinity. So, in the fifth and sixth centuries the words 'and the son' were added – *filio* meaning Son, '*que*' meaning 'and. For half a millennium the east and west tried to resist the urge to fight about the presence of *filioque*, but eventually, in 1054 the east had had enough. Not only did they disagree with the theology, it was Rome's arrogance and assumption that they were both right and able to dictate to their eastern cousins. Further events acted as charges to the main detonation, and eventually, the two parted ways. The division remained for centuries and is in place in many churches today. The east-west split, to some, appears impossible to repair. Rome (or Santiago) and Istanbul (or Moscow) may tolerate each other now, but their inability to share communion together highlights just how deep their division really is.

And yet, there has been change. What was heralded as The Great Emergence of the early twenty-first century marched underneath a variety of flags – and removing the *filioque* was one of them. The Emergents saw it as a symptom of the West's constriction of Christianity, and drove towards a broader view of the role, function and identity of the Holy Spirit. They were more than a little hated for it by some, but their message took root as it gradually became clear that they were not alone. After two thousand years of being the poor relation, the gradual removal of the *filioque* from formal liturgy was both a symptom and a cause of a fresh view of the Trinity.

1215
Magna Carta

1337 – 1453
The Hundred Years' War

c1300
Easter Island statues built

c1348
Black Death
reaches Europe

THE CRUSADES

I wish it wasn't so, but what followed was dark. The Church – so often plagued by corruption and stained with blood – was about to write a new chapter. It would have been better if none of what follows were true.

Having fallen to the Turks, Jerusalem was no longer a possible destination for Christian pilgrims. Pope Urban II resolved to rectify this, seeing it as an opportunity to unite a fractious Church. His sales pitch struck a chord with tens of thousands of peasants and noblemen who all agreed to join in and sign up for the epic adventure. Theirs was a holy mission, they believed, a direct command from God himself to liberate the birthplace of Christianity from Muslim hands. Surely they would be successful? If they weren't, could heaven be far off after their death?

As with all mobs, their ideals soon were left behind, trampled in the mud; what drove them was more like a lust for blood than a misguided sense of Godly duty. As the first hoards made their way east, travelling down through Hungary, any hint of divine mandate evaporated; they slaughtered Jews, murdered women and babies and ransacked towns even before reaching the enemy itself. When they finally faced the armies they had travelled so far to kill, the Turks made light work of their destruction.

A little while later, starting out in 1097, a more successful attack delivered Antioch to the Christians. The Turks also lost Jerusalem to its previous Arab owners, who once again opened the city up to pilgrims. Yet this was not enough for those hungry

800
Charlemagne becomes
Emperor

1096 – 1270
The Crusades

1173
Saladin becomes
Sultan of Egypt

1206
Genghis Khan founds
Mongol Empire

for more blood, loot and glory. In 1099, after atrocities that make the worst moments of the twentieth and twenty-first centuries read like child's fiction, Jerusalem was once more claimed for Christ. Quite whether he wanted that way it is another matter. Cannibalism, mass executions, the use of severed heads as missiles thrown over city walls, streets running deep with blood, Muslims cut open in search of swallowed treasure, Jews locked in their synagogues and burnt to death... there was nothing righteous about this Crusade.

Nor the next one. Nor the one after that. Nor any of the Crusades that followed. Over the following century-and-a-half Christian armies returned again and again to reclaim territories that were taken back by either Turks or Muslims.

While there were no specific Crusades against Jews – and for some time Church law had done much to prevent such anti-Semitic attacks – during the first three Crusades there were many incidents of Crusaders deliberately attacking Jews. Why? Well, since the trip was about history and the holy land, avenging the crucifixion of Christ became a significant motivation, and Jews made an obvious target.

To paint the Crusades as entirely devoid of integrity and honour is slightly misleading; there was one notable instance of righteous behaviour. It was in 1187, and capturing Jerusalem from the Arabs once more, the incoming commander treated those in the city with dignity and respect. He allowed his enemy's people to leave unharmed. His name was Saladin. He was a Muslim. Not only did he recapture many cities taken by the Christians in the Crusades,

Saladin managed to do it without stooping to the barbarisms of the other protagonists. His reputation grew and he was praised by the British King Richard I as the greatest and most powerful leader in the Islamic world. Returning the compliment, Saladin declared that no Christian leader was more honourable than Richard. Gifts were exchanged and a treaty signed in 1192. Under the terms of this treaty Jerusalem would remain in Muslim hands but be open to Christian pilgrimage.

A story from a year earlier adds a little more colour to Saladin's portrait. It was April and a European woman living in a camp near Saladin's home discovered that her three-month- old baby had been stolen and sold in the market. Her friends suggested she approach Saladin for help, which she did. He used his own money to buy the child and returned it to its mother. This generosity was typical, and explains why, when Saladin died two years later, aged 60, there was not enough money left behind to pay for his own funeral.

At the time they took place, the Crusades performed a vital role for many in Europe: the rescue of Christ's homeland. If they succeeded, then Christianity itself would benefit – or so the logic went. Wars may not be good for the soldiers who do the fighting and the dying, but engaging a common enemy can work wonders for the flagging support of home leaders. For some in Europe the Crusades were both a distraction from problems at home and an opportunity to create a stronger sense of unity. After all, if God is charging you with a task worth risking life and limb for, surely you must be doing something right?

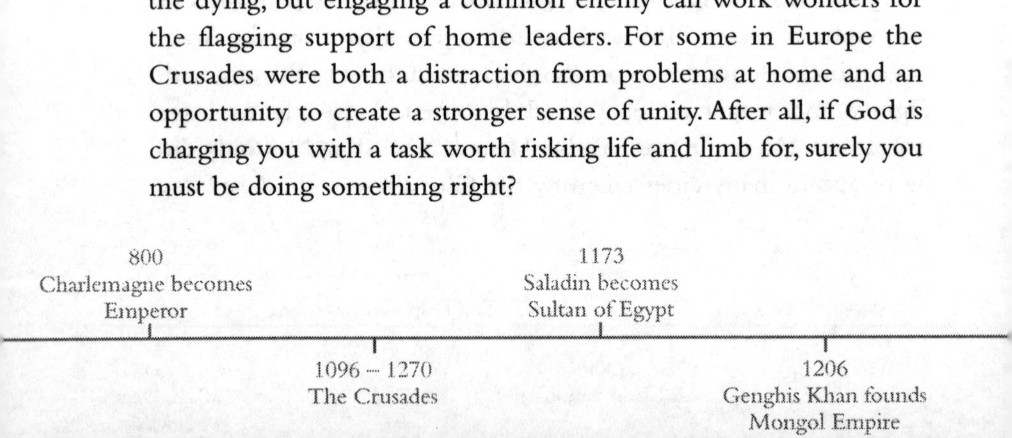

Many still point to these days as the seasons when the seeds of hatred were sown. Both Muslims and Jews trace much of their later oppression from this point, although anti-Semitism started long before with certain elements of the early Church. Neither have recovered from the 150 years of brutal torture at the hands of those professing to follow Christ. As for the Church itself, some suggest that it never fully recovered.

While those brutalised by the Christians' actions have always been clear about what the Crusades meant to them, the Church has not always been so transparent. For centuries afterwards the campaigns were either held up as examples of a righteous cause that had limited success, or were conveniently swept under the carpet. It was only in the twentieth century that the collective consciousness began to show any sign of remorse. And it was not until the mid-twenty-first century, when relations between Islam and Christianity had drastically deteriorated once more, that the drive for a full and formal apology gathered speed. Scholars may recall that in 2000 Pope John Paul II issued an apology for 'misdeeds' but his words were so clinically chosen as to have next to no impact. It would be years before the issue was addressed appropriately.

BLACKNESS AND DEATH

Whether its origins were in Africa or Asia, in rats or in humans, the Black Death – or bubonic plague – was perfectly clear in its outcome. Worldwide an estimated seventy-five million people lost their lives as their bodies haemorrhaged from within.

1215
Magna Carta

1337 – 1453
The Hundred Years' War

c1300
Easter Island statues built

c1348
Black Death reaches Europe

Between thirty to sixty per cent of Europe's population succumbed, most dying within four to seven days of infection. For over four hundred years Europe in particular was victim to its whimsical culling.

As the corpses began to stack up like pyramids, England and France embarked on their Hundred Years' War. Both countries had little to offer in the way of resistance, and malnutrition, disease and life-sapping poverty overwhelmed many. With a silent killer hovering like a Biblical plague, could there be any clearer sign that the world was about to end?

People looked around for a target they could blame. Jewish communities were high up on the list and in August of 1349 Jews in Mainz and Cologne were exterminated. This was not unusual; local Christians in Strasbourg had already murdered two thousand others earlier on in the year. Lepers, beggars, foreigners and anyone else who would present little in the way of defence also became a target, and gradually the warped mindset took hold: the plague was God's judgment and his anger must be appeased by the purging of the unclean.

In many ways the established Church suffered mightily during the plague. When it became clear that the men of God were just as powerless as the rest of the population to end the disease – while still claiming to be morally superior – revolt was not far off.

It came in a variety of forms. Some attacked those in religious authority, while others followed a new breed of preacher/evangelist/performance artist. If the problem was sin – and many believed that it was – then what better way to fix it than with a jolly good

800
Charlemagne becomes
Emperor

1173
Saladin becomes
Sultan of Egypt

1096 – 1270
The Crusades

1206
Genghis Khan founds
Mongol Empire

whipping? The so-called Flagellants travelled from town to town, emulating Christ's own final days of suffering and pain.

Some upped their financial support of the Church – in the hope that their funding would buy an easier passage out of the world – while others simply embraced hedonism with all the energy they could summon. Whatever the reaction, Europe was in a mess, and the Church was struggling to find a united voice that would offer comfort and leadership to those transfixed by the fear of the end of the world.

Sounds familiar, doesn't it? It's a pattern that we've seen since then; the world outside the Church finds that life lived according to its own agenda does not deliver them to paradise's door, so people look beyond themselves for a solution or something to help guide them. And what do they see when they look at the Church? That's the question.

Some will see Cluny and Aquinas and Anselm, or whoever it is around them that reflects just a little of the integrity, sacrifice and inspiration we should all crave. But many will see a Church characterised by self-interest, greed and violence. There have been too many Crusades over the years, too many chapters like this. For some we are characterised by our misdeeds, defined by our darkest moments. An unfair judgement? Who can really say what it is that we deserve?

So was the Church failing at this point? I'm sorry but I can't accept the premise of the question. Yes there were sins and errors and egregious problems crafted by the hands of the very people who were supposed to know – and behave – better. But failure? I don't

1215
Magna Carta

1337 – 1453
The Hundred Years' War

c1300
Easter Island statues built

c1348
Black Death reaches Europe

think the Church can be measured like that, with failure at one end and success at the other. It's only the grace of God that allows us to be here, isn't it? Do any of us even deserve to be a part of the Church?

Still, those Crusades represented a new low in the story of Christianity. And there were greater depths still to be plumbed.

Chapter Five

1399 – 1599

Sex! Corpse! Incest! Pope! Torture!

There are some lists that you really don't want to be on. We're not talking personal pollution ratings, genetic abnormalisms or inter-republic code violations; it's the big lists that really ought to be avoided. Like the ones for exceptional killers: The Most Prolific, The Most Depraved, The Top Ten Particularly Gruesome And Bizarre. Whatever the title, these are the sort of lists you really do not want to end up on. Especially when your father happens to be the Pope.

Somewhere towards the top of more than one of those lists – her crimes robbed just a little of their horror by the centuries that have passed – is Lucrezia Borgia, only daughter of Pope Alexander VI and his mistress. That's right, a mistress. But if marital infidelity among the Papacy shocks you, just wait until you digest what follows. The truth is that during these dark times the Popes allowed their moral authority to slip considerably. Perhaps that is why it is even rumoured that at one point a horse even made its way to the role. The rumour is false, but its mere presence hints at the difficulties within the papacy during those days.

If rumour is correct, Lucrezia's speciality was poison. She employed both a cook and a poisoner, had a hollow-ring in which she stored conveniently-accessed supplies of ordourless, tasteless arsenic, and was famed for dinner parties that were every bit as lethal as they were lavish. Such was her infamy that a joke from the Renaissance era remains; it was fashionable for many people around the Vatican to boast that they were going to dine with the Borgias that night. Considerably fewer were able to say that they had dined with them 'last night'.

Admittedly the humour has probably been diluted by time, and while Lucrezia Borgia's life is stained by rumour, there are elements of truth of which we can be rather more sure. Like the fact that her father

1429
Joan of Arc defeats
English at Orleans

1453
Fall of Constantinople

c1450
Incan city Machu Picchu built, Peru

1455
First Gutenberg Bible

– the epitome of papal corruption, vice and Machiavellian evil-doing of the time - was the driving force behind many of his daughter's crimes.

By the time she was eleven years old, Alexander – at that time merely Cardinal Rodrigo Borgia – had betrothed her twice, only to yank her back from marriage on both occasions. Once installed in the Vatican as head of the Holy Church, Pope Alexander VI married her off to Giovanni Sforza, cleverly forging an alliance with his powerful Milanese family. As new political alliances emerged over the passing years, the Sforza family eventually lost their importance to the Pope. And because Lucrezia knew her father to be a practical sort of man, she warned her husband that since he was no longer needed there was a good likelihood that he was about to be murdered. Wisely, he fled the city, which was good for Sforza but frustrating for the Pope; how could he benefit from marrying his daughter off to someone else again if she was still married? The only real option available to him was to have the marriage annulled, and the only possibility was if the marriage had not been consummated. But that brought up another problem; who would believe that his daughter had abstained from sex? Using a blend of intimidation and humiliation, Alexander eventually left Giovanni Sforza no choice but to agree to an annulment on the grounds that the reason for the marriage not being consummated was that he was impotent. Conveniently, Sforza agreed and Lucrezia was free again to marry, and once again to be used by Dad to secure politically convenient alliances.

Staying in a nearby convent, Lucrezia became pregnant, thanks to her liaison with Perotto, a young chamberlain. Later – still pregnant - Lucrezia took part in an audacious ceremony in which Vatican judges swore that she was *intacta*; that she remained a virgin. Despite rumours of incest between father and daughter, the Borgias continued to go on the offensive. Cesare – Lucrezia's brother – first stabbed Perotto, then had him thrown in prison and eventually arranged that he 'had fallen into the Tiber against his will'.

In an attempt to secure a future for her illegitimate son, Lucrezia pressed her father to issue two papal bulls (official documents), the first stating that the child was the offspring of Cesare and an unknown woman, the second stating that he was the son of the pope himself.

All this, and Lucrezia was still only seventeen.

She married the similarly youthful Prince of Aragon, Alfonso. Yet when this alliance lost its lustre for Pope Alexander, Alfonso was murdered. After a brief stint as the overseer of the administration of the Vatican and the Church, Lucrezia married for a final time – thanks to a deal brokered by her brother with the Prince and heir to the duchy of Ferrara.

Her life continued to flirt with scandal and tragedy in equal measure. The darker of the classic themes of Renaissance life wove their way in and out of her own; sexual gratification, lustrous art, syphilis, death. Her burial in the convent at Ferrara, Northern Italy, divides opinion: an ironic twist at the end of a godless life, or a final act of grace for a victim of so much greed and vice?

Of her father's legacy, however, we can be far surer. From the rumours of his having bought the papacy for five mule-loads of silver to the way he dragged his office away from any spiritual authority, down towards a gutter of greed and self-interest, Pope Alexander VI remains at the very bottom of the list of Great Popes.

Depending on how you take your history, his death in 1503 was either the result of accidental poisoning or a bout of malaria. Either way,

1429
Joan of Arc defeats English at Orleans

c1450
Incan city Machu Picchu built, Peru

1453
Fall of Constantinople

1455
First Gutenberg Bible

few wanted anything to do with the corpse. Not only was it decomposing at a rapid and intensely repulsive rate – reported by one official to be 'the ugliest, most monstrous and horrible dead body that was ever seen, without any form or likeness of humanity' – but Alexander's reputation had already caught up with him. His body was treated with utter disdain, having to be jumped upon by a worker struggling to wedge its swollen limbs into the undersized coffin. Things got worse at the funeral; the priests of St Peter's Basilica refused to accept the body for burial until forced to do so by the Vatican. The Requiem Mass was low on numbers and his successor – Pope Pius III - forbade the saying of a Mass for the man. After all, he said, 'it is blasphemous to pray for the damned'. Eventually the body was removed from the crypts of St Peter's and returned to Spain, Alexander's country of origin.

If he were the only one then perhaps this period in the history of Christianity would not be so bleak. Yet Alexander VI was just one in a long line of popes who appeared to be intent on driving the Church over a cliff. It wasn't even enough to embrace secularism; these *anti-popes* surrendered all claim to morality or personal integrity, their noses buried deep in corruption.

Twenty years before he became pontiff – and before Pope Innocent III who would sell you a decent title in the Church if the price was right – Alexander's shoes were warmed by Pope Sixtus IV, by all accounts a clever man who managed to behave like a complete fool. Not only did he wage war against the Turks as well as the Florentines, appoint his relatives to high office and appoint as bishops those men who paid him with sexual favours, Sixtus also was involved in a failed assassination attempt of a local ruler.

1480
Spanish Inquisition begins

1498
Leonardo Da Vinci's
The Last Supper

1520 – 1566
Sulayman the Magnificent
rules Ottoman Empire

1527
Sack of Rome

But it was his support of the formation of the Spanish Inquisition – support that, admittedly, did waver from time to time – that stands out. Charged with the task of rooting out undesirable elements from within the Catholic Church, Sixtus went after the Jews, Protestants and any other type of traitor that he fancied.

The Inquisition was meant to ensure that new Christian converts were in possession of the correct teaching on key doctrinal issues. Yet it routinely used torture as a means of forcing confessions from its victims. Of the three favoured methods, the *garrucha* saw the victim suspended from the ceiling by his ankles, with weights used to lift, drop and leave the limbs dislocated. The *potro* – known throughout the English speaking world simply as The Rack – was the most popular. The victims we placed upon it and their limbs pulled in opposite directions. First they were dislocated, then separated, the muscle and cartilage, ligaments or bones eventually giving way and snapping. Pushed to the extreme, the limbs could be pulled off completely. The *toca*, meanwhile, was a simpler affair; a rag stuffed in the mouth and water poured over the restrained head did wonders for loosening the tongues of those with a fear of drowning. The *toca* remains popular to this day, despite international outcry against its modern cousin, waterboarding.

All along while these tortures were administered, the priests would be standing by, directing operations. For those who resisted the above, the trial would follow and lead them, likely as not, to the excruciating death while tethered to a burning stake.

A similar end awaited Girolamo Savonarola; executed in public in Florence in 1498. Long time critic of Pope Alexander VI, Savonarola

1429
Joan of Arc defeats English at Orleans

1453
Fall of Constantinople

c1450
Incan city Machu Picchu built, Peru

1455
First Gutenberg Bible

railed against the moral decay that infected the Church. His list of targets was long: homosexuality, pagan books, immoral sculptures, lewd pictures, gaming tables, mirrors, cosmetics, chess pieces, lutes and other musical instruments, fine dresses, women's hats, and the works of immoral and ancient poets. As leader of what he called the *Christian and Religious Republic of Florence* he wanted all such items to be collected and burned in one of the public squares, forming the so-called Bonfire of Vanities.

His death in the same square a year later was a sign that the Pope had finally got his way and silenced his critic. However unpalatable Savonarola's fundamentalism may have been, he had a point; the Church was heading in the wrong direction and something had to be done.

Take a look around any collection of art from the period of the Italian Renaissance and, at times, it is possible to sense God working to combat the inadequacies of his Church through the medium of art. Leonardo da Vinci redefined not only what it meant to be a man of many talents, but he also found ways of appealing to the masses on a profoundly spiritual level.

In fact, art might just be the one path for redemption open to the memory of Sixtus IV; his commissioning of the Sistine Chapel opened up the canvas on which Michelangelo would paint the Creation of Adam. Fra Angelico – a man who must have picked up the nicknames 'the Blessed' and 'the Angelic One' for a reason - had painted with such a sense of intimacy that surely all cannot have been lost among the faithful? A century or so later and, with the Renaissance spreading out from Rome with incredible intensity, Flemish painter Peter Paul Rubens unveiled *The Entombment*; a work of such power and inspiration that few could doubt that God remained a lover of fine art.

Like all things, man's desire to point the finger of blame leads us into trouble. Art was no more the cause of the moral decline than the Spanish Inquisition was an effective remedy for theological failings. Like all tools, the moral value of art depended on the hand from which it came. Those with an interest in re-examining classical traditions found themselves the subject of scorn and criticism from the religious elite. Others were able to use their skills to draw people's focus towards God.

It has always been this way, and probably always will be. Books, songs, images and films will continue to be banned and the arguments about whether these are merely the symptoms of a changing morality or the actual cause will continue to rage all around them. As long as the Church continues to travel in the opposite direction to that charted by the trio of popes at the end of the fifteenth century, we might just have a chance of being listened to when we join in the debate.

THE LIBRARY

At this point we need to jump back a little. By the end of the first century all the texts that would eventually make up the New Testament had been written, yet which books and letters would be included remained a subject for debate. Written in Greek upon the crushed, flattened and thinned out stalks of papyrus reed, twenty-four of the final twenty- seven were typically agreed upon, but Jude, 2 Peter and Revelation did not make their way into the canon until AD 315 in Alexandria. Similarly, Paul's letter to the Church at Laodicea was pulled from the list. Eventually Athenasius, Alexandria's bishop at the time identified the twenty-seven books which have been recognised ever since as the complete collection of New Testament Scripture.

1429
Joan of Arc defeats English at Orleans

c1450
Incan city Machu Picchu built, Peru

1453
Fall of Constantinople

1455
First Gutenberg Bible

Incidentally, of the original Greek-language copies that survive today, there are almost six thousand, with almost twenty-five thousand ancient copies translated into other languages. There are just six hundred original surviving copies of Homer's Iliad, making the New Testament by far the best surviving ancient text to this day.

Jerome, in 382, finally translated the New Testament from Greek to Latin, including the fourteen books of historical Jewish writing known as the Old Testament Apocrypha. He scribbled a note to indicate that he was unsure quite whether these additional texts were inspired spiritual writings, yet they caused little controversy; the Old Testament Apocrypha were included in the Bible until the final years of the nineteenth century, when the Protestants finally got their way and yanked them out.

It wasn't the first time that Scripture's power prompted heavy handed responses from Church leaders. Around 500 there were as many as fifty translations of the Bible in official use. A century later and the Church had seen to it that there was just one; Jerome's original Latin version.

The reasons for the cut-back are not hard to imagine – especially when you add in the knowledge that possession of a non-Latin Bible was a crime punishable by execution. Control of Scripture allowed control of the message, and control of the message made raising money and directing behaviour far, far easier.

It would have worked too if it wasn't for those isolated communes like the one found on the remote Scottish island of Iona. With their opposition to the Roman Catholic Church, these communes remained a dim yet consistent light beneath the brooding skies of the Dark and Middle Ages. Eventually, their seven-hundred-year opposition to Papal authority inspired open rebellion. John Wycliffe, scholar, theologian

1480
Spanish Inquisition begins

1527
Sack of Rome

1498
Leonardo Da Vinci's
The Last Supper

1520 – 1566
Sulayman the Magnificent
rules Ottoman Empire

and man with more than a few skills when it came to Latin-English translation, finally wrestled the text away from its Rome-based masters. Of course, none of this went down too well and even forty-four years after his death the Pope demanded that Wycliffe's bones be dug up, burnt to ash and hurled into the unconsecrated river nearby.

Theology and technology became close friends thanks to a man with the skin of a bird. Johann Gensfleisch (translation: John Gooseflesh) knew the power of words. He opted to change his name to the far more appealing Johann Gutenberg (translation: John Beautiful Mountain) and invented what was perhaps the most single most significant tool in the whole history of Christianity. As the 1450s unwound, his movable-type printing press allowed Bibles – and other books – to be produced in large quantities in a short period of time. The fact that his judgment was such that he ended up impoverished due to some unscrupulous business associates only adds to the sense that somehow Guttenberg's work had more than a little divine intervention in it.

Back to Wycliffe. His bones were dug up in 1428, but it was too late to stop the flow of change. A series of reformers took the mantle upon themselves to bring Scripture back to the masses and set it as the compass for Christian living.

One of the earliest reformers to take Wycliffe's teachings to heart - Jan Hus - had already paid for his vocal opposition to Rome's rule with his life. Born in Bohemia, Hus was burned at the stake in 1415, with the cruelly creative touch of Wycliffe's manuscript Bibles being used as kindling for the fire. As the flames began to eat into his flesh Hus offered up his final words: 'In 100 years, God will raise up a man whose calls for reform cannot be suppressed.'

He was only out by two years.

Chapter Six

1521 – 1579 Rolling out the Protestant Reformation

Something had to give. Mired in corruption, neutered by greed and self-interest, the Church needed help. It needed saving from itself.

Help came in the shape of a summer's evening, a thunderstorm and a fearful twenty-one- year-old German disenchanted with his future career as a lawyer. As Martin Luther witnessed a bolt of lightning strike near him as he returned from home to the University of Erfurt – a place he later condemned for being little more than a 'beerhouse and a whorehouse' – he wondered if this was his final moment. Was this storm about to take his life? Was it some form of divine judgement served up for a life less than worthy? Panicking, Luther took the path which made the most sense, making the only bargain he could in the hope of sparing his life; he swore that if he should make it home alive he would become a monk.

Martin Luther, though young, was a man of his word. Within six weeks he had sold his books and enrolled in an Augustine monastery in Erfurt, despite the fact that he appeared less than convinced about the wisdom of his decision. Marked by his sorrowful demeanour, Luther's farewell supper with his university friends ended with the words: 'This day you see me, and then, not ever again.'

Thankfully, Luther's integrity outpaced his prophetic skills. Far from retreating into a world of silence and anonymity, he eventually became one of the dominant thinkers of the second millennium. He helped the Church to wake up to itself, emerging from the disturbed slumber of previous years. Luther ended up both as Protestantism's midwife and as yet another in a long line of judges who spoke out against the wayward failings of God's followers.

But none of this happened without him first wading through a

1506 – 1612
St Peter's Basilica built, Rome

1517
Martin Luther posts his *95 Theses*

1524 – 1525
The Peasants' War

1536
John Calvin's *Institutes of the Christian Religion*

prolonged period of doubt and spiritual crisis. Luther's early years as a monk were coloured in by an increasing sense of dissatisfaction. Plenty of prayer, confession and pilgrimage only served to reinforce in his own mind just how wretched he was. Indeed, later on in life he reflected on this period as one in which he 'lost hold of Christ the Saviour and Comforter and made of him a stock-master and hangman over my poor soul'. Regularly confessing his sins a reported twenty-one times a day, Luther was plagued by a fear of dying with unconfessed sin dogging his eternal prospects.

The change in him came over time. While developing a particular affinity for the Psalms, as well as the books of Romans, Hebrews and Galatians, Luther began to question the Catholic Church's interpretation of the doctrine of justification. At the time, the official line was that righteous acts – or righteousness itself - were the result of cooperation between God and man. In other words, individuals' behaviour played a part in their salvation, or that part of the credit went to us as well as to God. If the people would only behave in the right way – following the rules and performing procedures with sufficient skill (and, by the way, offering the correct financial gifts in the process) – then enough boxes would have been ticked in order to ensure salvation.

Luther thought otherwise, and he had Romans 3:21–26 on his side. He suggested that in fact it was all due to God and God alone that one can be saved, redeemed or counted as worthy of Christ's sacrifice. Justification, he echoed, came by God's grace which was ours through faith, not works.

This went to the heart of much of the corruption that plagued the

1538
Henry VIII breaks
from Rome

1549
First *Book of Common Prayer*

1545
The Council of Trent

1570
Elizabeth I
excommunicated

Church in the fifteenth and sixteenth centuries. Of the possible illustrations of quite how bad things had become, the selling of indulgences is one of the clearest – even if it lacks the brutal sensationalism of other episodes. The deal was simple: in an attempt to raise funds for a building project (St Peter's Church in Rome) Pope Leo X took the unusual step in 1517 of selling 'indulgences'; granting absolution for sins in return for cash. It was a special offer of forgiveness made at a bargain price. For a little bit more money, individuals were allowed to indulge in a continuous lifestyle of sin. That's right, friends: keep that mistress and be guilt-free! Worried about Purgatory? Uncomfortable with the notion of having to deal with lifestyle consequences after death? Don't worry: the Church will sell you salvation not only for your own soul, but your loved ones' too!

Sixteenth-century marketing guru Johann Tetzel is even said at the time to have come up with a slogan: 'As soon as the coin in the coffer rings, the soul from purgatory springs.' Pope Leo added to the scandal by claiming: 'The fable of Christ has been quite profitable to us!'

It's not hard to see why Luther got so worked up.

And when his flock arrived at confession brandishing their indulgences – printed on paper and freshly purchased, they began to question whether there was any need for them to even repent of their sins at all. Why should they bother when the pre-paid document in their hand promised to forgive all sins?

Luther's response was pure theatre. Committing his thoughts to paper, he wrote *The 95 Theses* – a series of statements running to a

1506 – 1612
St Peter's Basilica built, Rome

1517
Martin Luther posts his *95 Theses*

1524 – 1525
The Peasants' War

1536
John Calvin's *Institutes of the Christian Religion*

little over 2,500 words questioning the sale of indulgences: the 'holy trade' as it was becoming known. Yet even though his words were not designed to ignite a revolution – Luther's aim was to discuss the issues rather than erase them – they were the spark that lit the forest fire. Some say he nailed his document to the doors of the church in Wittenberg, others say he mailed them to the Bishop. Either way, the word about the statements spread rapidly, gaining massive popularity among believers of all social standing, degrees of wealth and background.

And so begins the story of Protestantism, a story still being written six hundred years later. It is a journey that started with Luther's rejection of the Church's self-interest and continued initially for more than a century with the Reformation, a period that involved kings and popes and courts and which, in the process, forced Luther to take cover for fear of retribution. It was a muscular period, one of change and boldness and disagreement. It was a strange period too, made even stranger by the names that echo down the centuries: Wittenberg (the town borrowed by Shakespeare for Hamlet's education), the Black Band (a group of mercenaries loyal to Pope Leo) and the Diet of Worms (a protracted conference or *Diet*, held in Worms, a small town on the Rhine)which condemned Luther as a heretic. Yet Luther's heroic words as he faced his accusers sound louder than any of the curiosities;

'Here I stand. I can do no other. God help me. Amen.'

Aside from the headlines and the history, Luther's influence on Christianity and believers the world over is of huge significance. The Gutenberg Bible may have been in print since the previous century

1538
Henry VIII breaks from Rome

1545
The Council of Trent

1549
First *Book of Common Prayer*

1570
Elizabeth I excommunicated

but it was Luther who revolutionised the part the Bible plays within the Christian faith. His teaching drove believers back towards the personal, away from the corporate, finding truth and direct revelation from God within Scripture, instead of through the hierarchy of Church leadership.

Until Luther and his contemporaries spoke out, the role of the Bible for the Church has been a rather muted one. Hardly ever read, it was subservient to tradition, form and ritual. Only popes and saints and councils had the authority to interpret Scripture, leaving the religious masses ignorant of its content and immune from its challenges.

But not Luther. Having spent years performing acts of spiritual sacrifice and discipline, he realised that such activities brought him no closer to God. What's more, they only served to compound the problem, sending out a message that our human ability to get us closer to God is barely of any worth at all. His understanding of God and faith followed a different path. Immersing himself in Scripture, his teaching was the result of the personal conviction that followed his reading of God's book. In his mind there were clear, logical steps that formed the essence of the Christian journey; God communicates solely through Scripture, which can only truly be read by those who have received the gift of faith. Far from being a personal achievement, Luther saw faith as another example of God's enduring goodness. Always good, always just, always beyond our comprehension; Luther's view of God placed him both beyond us yet also – by grace – beside us. Despite our sinful nature, the birth, death and resurrection of Christ proves once and for all that it is by

1506 – 1612
St Peter's Basilica built, Rome

1524 – 1525
The Peasants' War

1517
Martin Luther posts his *95 Theses*

1536
John Calvin's *Institutes of the Christian Religion*

God's grace that we are redeemed, not by our own efforts and abilities.

This did not go down well.

According to Luther and the body of fellow reform-minded scholars, theologians and preachers – of whom more a little later on – the fact that God had sent his son to die for the sins of humankind had massive implications. There was no need for a mediator, whether that be saints of old interceding for us, priests atoning for us or the Virgin Mary mediating for us. Returning to the message of earlier theologians, relying once again on the Bible for revelation – Scripture through which God reveals himself, rather than through which he is discovered – the reformers swept away a faith cluttered with paraphernalia, from shrines and rosaries to Holy Water and significant stones. This was the time of the emergence of the *sola scriptura* doctrine; the assertion that the Bible as God's written word is self-authenticating, clear and enough by itself to be taken as the final authority of Christian doctrine.

Sola scriptura remains foundational for Protestantism today, just as Roman Catholic, Eastern Orthodox and Oriental Orthodox Churches teach that the Scriptures are an important but not exclusive part of the sacred tradition from which the Churches derive their doctrines. They believe that the Church has authority over the Scriptures by virtue of the fact that it actively selected which books were to be in the biblical canon. Protestants, on the other hand, believe the Church merely recognised and received the books that were already widely considered canonical.

With that same spirit of reorganisation, the Reformers dragged

1538
Henry VIII breaks from Rome

1545
The Council of Trent

1549
First *Book of Common Prayer*

1570
Elizabeth I excommunicated

Christianity back from its meanderings, hoping to return it to a path far closer to that laid out by Christ himself.

Luther became the most widely read author in Germany, and his translation of the Bible – written while hiding in a castle, suffering from constipation and calling himself George – established a new precedent by removing the Jewish historical writings collected in the Old Testament Apocrypha. Once out of hiding he found that his early actions had sparked considerable developments; churches were hosting services in German rather than Latin, with both bread and now wine available to all. Ministers were marrying, wearing plain clothes and cutting down on the icons, fast days and masses for the dead.

The ideals spread north, inspiring Danes and Swedes frustrated by overseas leaders imposing unpopular rules. As well as fighting criticism from the right, Luther also was criticised as being too conservative by Thomas Muntzer, a preacher who, bizarrely, would later feature on banknotes in communist East Germany. Still, back in the sixteenth century Muntzer was less preoccupied with his status as pin-up and more concerned that Luther's reforms were not going far enough. Muntzer felt that there was too much clutter with Church leaders involved, and that believers should be able to throw off their spiritual and political leaders. He encouraged open revolt against monasteries and castles, which seemed to go relatively well until the showdown known as the Battle of Frankenhausen. With as many as 8,000 peasants alongside him, Muntzer claimed that God would intervene and guarantee their victory. Unfortunately he was wrong and the rabble was comprehensively defeated, the final casualty

1506 – 1612
St Peter's Basilica built, Rome

1517
Martin Luther posts his *95 Theses*

1524 – 1525
The Peasants' War

1536
John Calvin's *Institutes of the Christian Religion*

figures ending up as a heavily one-sided 3,000:6. Muntzer was captured, imprisoned and tortured, after which he was prepared to recant, accept the Roman Catholic mass and have his head chopped off.

It was a brutal end for the leader of the so-called Peasants' War, yet Muntzer's influence was not fully eliminated. Others followed in his footsteps and formed the Anabaptist wing of the Church. Logically, they concluded that since there were no instances of infant baptism in the Bible – and since faith was required in order to access salvation – pretty much everyone who professed belief in Christ was in need of rebaptising. And as for all those old authority figures in the Church; well, they simply had to go. Anabaptists preferred collective rule rather than top-down leadership, radically influencing future concepts of the involvement of congregations in the life of their religious communities. If only they hadn't opted to reinstate the Old Testament law of polygamy they may well have enjoyed even greater popularity.

Anabaptism did not go down well – in general its followers were considered to be dangerous, over-zealous hot-heads – but it did have the effect of reuniting Catholics with Luther's emergent Protestant movement, especially when the Anabaptist polygamists took control of the German city of Munster for eighteen months. The party ended with mass, public executions and the corpses of the leaders displayed in cages hung from the steeple of St Lambert's Church. All that zealous rebellion brought them death and infamy, yet still they remained popular in certain corners.

Meanwhile, reformation fever was catching on in England, where the XXXL-sized King Henry VIII was having trouble producing a

1538
Henry VIII breaks from Rome

1545
The Council of Trent

1549
First *Book of Common Prayer*

1570
Elizabeth I excommunicated

male heir by his wife Catherine of Aragon. Ignoring Papal rule, he divorced and traded her in for a younger model, in the process positioning himself as the head of the Church in England. So began a division between Protestant and Catholic that would plague the country for decades to come.

Henry was clever enough to know that his new Church would need some serious legitimacy. He couldn't just execute his way through the opposition – although he gave it a good try. By appointing Thomas Cranmer as Archbishop of Canterbury he was able to witness the birth of a fully Protestant Church rather than a scaled down Roman import. Ironically, Henry's tastes may well have been more closely aligned to those of the pre-Reformation leaders of the Roman Catholic Church, yet under Cranmer's influence the Church of England became increasingly Protestant, despite initial teething problems. However, Cranmer paid for it with his life once the Catholic Queen 'Bloody' Mary settled on the throne in 1553.

As the balance of power shifted back to the emerging Anglican Church, it became clear that the project was far from complete. Some were quite happy to be considered Catholic so long as the *Roman* part was eliminated. Others pushed back with a clear call for Protestant ideals, and further division was sown.

THE REACTION

This was not what Luther wanted; the Catholic Church found itself being pulled apart like the bodies of those it had abused upon the rack in Spain. Pope Paul III was not indifferent to the events taking place across Europe, and launched his own parallel reforms to root

1506 – 1612
St Peter's Basilica built, Rome

1517
Martin Luther posts his *95 Theses*

1524 – 1525
The Peasants' War

1536
John Calvin's *Institutes of the Christian Religion*

out corruption and abuse. His 1545 council at Trento, northern Italy, lasted for years – longer than both he and Martin Luther. It failed to pull back the shifting plates of theology, but what force could have stopped the split? The Council rejected *sola scriptura* – the Protestant line that the Bible was the sole source of doctrine – and it was clear that the Church, so the council claimed, was not going to give up its authority so easily. History judges the result of the Council in different ways, with some suggesting that its rulings on the authority of the Pope, the veneration of the Virgin Mary, the existence of purgatory and the importance of relics made this a Greatest Hits of the Roman Catholic Church with all the classics repackaged, polished up and rolled out. Yet while Catholic doctrine was unchanged, issues of behaviour were dealt with fully. Corruption in many of its forms was tackled, although a muted form of indulgence-selling did remain. What is beyond dispute, however, is that the Church that emerged from Trent was utterly unrecognisable compared to that which had existed a couple of centuries earlier. The truth is that the Reformation impacted on all wings of the Church, not just those loyal to Protestant reform. Rome embraced what it could of Luther's work, disagreed on some points, but grew in integrity and strength as a result.

THE NEXT ONE

If it had not been for John Calvin, the wealthy televangelist dinosaurs of the late-twentieth centuries would have struggled to fuel their fleets of luxury cars. Not that Calvin's integrity was as questionable as the likes of Benny Hinn, Jimmy Swaggart et al – in fact, it would

1538
Henry VIII breaks from Rome

1545
The Council of Trent

1549
First *Book of Common Prayer*

1570
Elizabeth I excommunicated

be hard to find two schools of thought more widely separated. Yet it remains one of the stranger truths that the two are connected; such is the influence of the sixteenth- century lawyer that there are traces of his DNA in the most unlikely of places. It's in those rock-solid genes of personal thrift, hard work and, yes, the concept of material success as evidence of God's blessing that Calvin's legacy lived on to find unlikely ancestors.

Whether Calvin was destined for greatness is another matter, but it certainly seems as if his arrival in Geneva in 1536 was abnormally well-timed. The city had been the backdrop to some significant events during previous months, and change was heavy in the air. A colleague of Luther – Ulrich Zwingli – had encouraged followers to adopt a more radical approach to Catholicism. Luther was warm, affable and happy to concede that there was still some shared ground between Rome and the emerging Protestants when it came to the Eucharist. While he might not have gone as far as believing in transubstantiation – the assumption that the bread and wine turn literally into the body and blood of Christ himself during communion, despite remaining as bread and wine to the senses – he did acknowledge that the body of Jesus was present in the procedure.

For Zwingli this was not good enough. He encouraged a split from the German Lutheran movement, urging Protestant Reformers to drive further changes home. While he paid for his convictions with his life (fighting Swiss Catholics in 1531), Zwingli's message was not buried with him. In 1534 Reformed leaders encouraged a full-scale revolt against Catholic Churches throughout the Swiss city of Geneva. Mobs did what mobs are best at; smashing expensive

1506 – 1612
St Peter's Basilica built, Rome

1517
Martin Luther posts his *95 Theses*

1524 – 1525
The Peasants' War

1536
John Calvin's *Institutes of the Christian Religion*

artefacts to pieces. Altars, icons and statues all were burned, smashed and crushed.

Arriving in the city in 1536, Calvin was not impressed. It wasn't the chaos or the destruction that bothered him particularly – although there were elements of it that gave the lawyer cause to think. What troubled him more was the fact that if this was reform, then it simply wasn't enough.

According to Calvin, all that had really been achieved was a thorough refurb of Catholic Churches; rooting out and destroying icons and idols. True reformation was about far more than mere aesthetics. For the rest of his life – excluding a three-year period when he was exiled from the city – Calvin worked to make Geneva a model of Reformation in action. Clergy helped out with the governing, overseeing both private and public morality.

The Reformed Geneva was no theocratic police state. Calvin advanced theological understanding by developing a fresh call to believers. Theirs was a spiritual quest, one that should see them withdraw from carnal desires and elevate their ambitions to a wholly *spiritual* worship of God. Such worship needed no material objects to help it along; the physical could only obscure the spiritual, Calvin argued. There was plenty to get excited about too; Calvin argued that God's divinity was such that human destiny was entirely in his hands. For the few that were chosen, this was understandably good news. Those on the outside might have thought otherwise.

Still, the Reformation continued. Ironically enough, even though Aristotle and his kind were distinctly out of favour with the Reformers – Luther calling him a 'pagan rascal' – the shift away from

1538
Henry VIII breaks from Rome

1545
The Council of Trent

1549
First *Book of Common Prayer*

1570
Elizabeth I excommunicated

the 'physical' towards the 'spiritual' was another step in Christianity's journey away from its Jewish roots. By widening the divide still further, the Reformation was continuing in the tradition of Greek scholars who elevated the spiritual way above that which is merely human. Like all journeys towards single-sided opinions, this one would encounter problems for many centuries to come.

We see it today, just as we have experienced it in the past. According to writer Marvin R Wilson, the problem is that we read a Jewish book through the eyes of Greek culture. The rational, dualistic world of Greek philosophy struggles when it meets Jewish spirituality; even the very notion of what it means to be 'spiritual' causes great division. For the Jewish mindset, the term cannot be separated from the physical world. For the Greeks, the two cannot be far enough apart.

Of course, it is hardly surprising that the two schools drifted apart – just as the Reformation now seems to be steeped in a sense of inevitability. Christianity's relationship with its Jewish parents has always been troubled, yet the separation has not been easy – or, for that matter, particularly helpful.

Chapter Seven

1459 – 1769 The World Gets Bigger

Did Calvin kill the doctor? According to some he did. Depending on your politics Michael Servetus, a Spanish medic, was either bold or foolish. He condemned infant baptism, picked holes in the Trinity, suggested that Calvin should be sacked and graciously offered to look after his wealth on his behalf. Whatever the opinion of Servetus's ideas, *el médico* paid with his life as he was burned at the stake in Geneva some time in 1553.

For some, Calvin's memory takes the blame. After all, they suggest, it was in his town that the episode took place and the death sentence was something that the lawyer-turned-theologian approved. Yet, as we shall find out, Calvin was less guilty than he might first appear, and, besides; if this was his pitch to be remembered as a bloodthirsty tyrant, the appetite was clearly lacking as he didn't try to do it again.

Servetus had been condemned by Catholic France for what amounted to the same crimes as those that Calvin judged him for. It was perhaps more the efficiency of Genevan rule that caught him out rather than any tyrannical desire for control. Calvin made sure that he received the written support of all but one of the Protestant leaders and suggested that Servetus be offered a slightly less painful death beneath the axe rather than in the middle of flames. However, the Genevan council wanted to make a point, so the pyre was built and Calvin's reputation as a man who meant business was firmly cemented.

Like Calvin, Luther's influence was far from over. For both men, the grave itself was little more than a minor interruption before normal service was resumed. Luther's legacy of justification through faith, rather than faith plus works remains significant to this day.

1492
Christopher Columbus reaches America

1503
First African slaves taken to America

1572
St Bartholomew's Day Massacre

1577 – 1580
Francis Drake sails around world

Calvin's doctrine of predestination remains one of the key things that people know about him. Despite the fact that Luther shared many of his opinions, it is Calvin's notion of 'double predestination' – the idea that as well as God selecting those who were to be saved, he also earmarks those who are to be eternally damned – that continues to make the headlines.

At the start of the sixteenth century there was just one main expression of the Church in the West: Roman Catholicism. A century later and there were four. The Roman Catholics remained potent in the southern parts of Europe, the Lutherans ruled up in northern Germany and Scandinavia, England was under the power of the Anglican Church while the Reformed Churches dominated Switzerland, the Netherlands and Scotland.

Calvin's theology and practise had found a particularly responsive population among the Scots; John Knox – a former student of the man himself – brought Calvinism back to Scotland. Aiming for a more authentically New Testament mode of operation, Knox and his fellow believers ditched the power pyramid of bishops and remote rulers, opting instead for representation from the ground on up. Churches were run by their members – the presbyters – and the Presbyterian Church was born. If it hadn't been for their penchant for armed uprising then perhaps their New Testament credentials may have remained a little more intact. However, it was their very willingness to fight for their independence that kept them from being absorbed by either Anglican or Catholic power.

South of the border in England there were further divisions taking place within the Church. Henry VIII's bold move had failed to placate those reformers who were hungry for change. Protestantism was split; on one side were the Puritans who wanted the Church to absorb greater influence from the other European Reformers. The Anglicans disagreed, and started to see themselves as a middle ground between those who hailed Luther and Calvin on one hand and those who followed Rome on the other. The contention often boiled down to issues of style, with Protestants unhappy about the presence of robes, ornaments and tokens of wealth in general appearing in the Church. The Anglicans – some now Anglo-Catholic – borrowed from the past as they saw fit.

These Puritans gave birth to further Churches, often emerging out of a movement tagged as Separatist. John Smyth started down a path that was previously beaten by the Anabaptists – although Smyth's own Baptist Church had the benefit of not petrifying most people who took a closer look. Both emphasised the importance of baptism and questioned whether infant baptism was the real deal. Some of the emerging Baptists were hardcore Calvinists, while others looked back to the influence of Dutch theologian Jacob Arminius. He had issues with the notion of predestination, yet Arminianism was condemned by some as being a little too close to Catholicism. Still, certain Baptists appreciated it and Holland became something of a safe-haven for those whose views were a little too controversial.

As well as the emerging two camps of General and Particular Baptists there were the Quakers – named after their frequently twitchy, emotional and agitated state during meetings. Founded by the visionary George Fox, they represented a radical departure form business as usual. For the Quakers the notion of creating fresh theology

1492
Christopher Columbus reaches America

1503
First African slaves taken to America

1572
St Bartholomew's Day Massacre

1577 – 1580
Francis Drake sails around world

was not a matter of redefining the sacraments; it meant re-defining the very nature of humanity itself. Fox believed that all humans were touched by the Divine and therefore all humans had potential to access God. Churches suddenly seemed rather less important. Priests were significantly demoted. And Fox was in trouble.

Imprisoned frequently throughout his life, Fox was a man ahead of his time. Yes, the Quakers grew rapidly, with 100,000 members within a decade of Fox's death, but these were not the ripest of days for a true social revolutionary. Had Fox been born a couple (or even four) centuries later there is every chance that he would have achieved even more.

These were days of violence and war. The sixteenth and seventeenth centuries played host to a horrific glut of murders in the name of God. In France the Wars of Religion saw Catholic fight against Calvinist Huguenot, with perhaps the worst incident taking place in 1572. King Charles IX signed off on the assassination of certain Huguenot leaders while they were attending a wedding in Paris. The strike was anything but surgical. For three days a mob hunted Protestants and left a trail of corpses behind them. The fever spread, and for months the killing frenzy continued, until some 20,000 Protestants had been killed.

The Thirty Years War carried on the tradition, with English, French, Dutch and German states pitted against Spain and the Holy Roman Empire. Famine and disease increased the death toll, and by the end of the affair the power of the Holy Roman Empire was emaciated, Spain was on its knees, and the map of Protestant states looked like a pre-school exercise in splatter-painting.

1600 – 1614
East India Companies formed

1620
Mayflower leaves Plymouth

1618 – 1648
The Thirty Years' War

1754 – 1763
Anglo-French War, North America

England had not escaped fighting, with a Civil War drawing to a close at roughly the same time. With victory awarded to Oliver Cromwell and his fellow Protestant soldiers, for a handful of years they transformed England into a Commonwealth, banned theatres, sport on Sundays and swearing. It didn't last, of course. These were the days when violence seemed almost magnetic, as if society would only be allowed to drift so far towards peace before it found itself getting pulled back – regardless of will – towards violence and hatred.

THE WORLD AS WE KNEW IT

'Measure what is measurable, make measurable what is not so.'

These are the words of Galileo Galilei. He knew about immovable objects too, having repeatedly taken on the Church.

To be fair, it wasn't all Galileo's fault. It was Copernicus who started it. In the early sixteenth century the young Prussian published an incendiary work. He suggested that the earth was not the centre of the universe. Instead he suggested that it might just be the sun that played the bigger role in all this spinning around.

The Church was troubled by this. Considerably troubled, it turned out. Placing the earth at the very centre of the universe was a key building block. It was one of those essentials that simply could not be tossed away on a whim.

When the theories failed to evaporate, the Church in Rome eventually convened a board of theologians in 1616 to deal with the Copernican theory one and for all. The result was unambiguous and direct; to declare that the sun is at the centre of the universe (as well as that it is immovable) can only be described as 'foolish and absurd'

1492
Christopher Columbus reaches America

1503
First African slaves taken to America

1572
St Bartholomew's Day Massacre

1577 – 1580
Francis Drake sails around world

and 'formally heretical'. What's more, saying that the earth moves at all is pure foolishness and utterly 'erroneous in the faith'. Why, it even says so in Scripture:

> On the day the Lord gave the Amorites over to Israel, Joshua said to the Lord in the presence of Israel:
> 'O sun, stand still over Gibeon,
> O moon, over the Valley of Aijalon.'
>
> So the sun stood still,
> and the moon stopped,
> till the nation avenged itself on its enemies,
> as it is written in the Book of Jashar.
> The sun stopped in the middle of the sky and delayed going down about a full day. There has never been a day like it before or since, a day when the Lord listened to a man. Surely the Lord was fighting for Israel!'
>
> Joshua 10:12–14

It wasn't just those power-hungry Catholics who had issues; Calvin slated Copernicus's findings, and Martin Luther dropped a comment about it while dining one day:

'People gave ear to an upstart astrologer who strove to show that the earth revolves, not the heavens or the firmament, the sun and the moon ... This fool wishes to reverse the entire science of astronomy; but sacred Scripture tells us that Joshua commanded the sun to stand still, and not the earth.'

1600 – 1614
East India Companies formed

1620
Mayflower leaves Plymouth

1618 – 1648
The Thirty Years' War

1754 – 1763
Anglo-French War, North America

The fact was that the earth was at the centre of the universe and anyone who said otherwise was a fool.

Unfortunately, they weren't so foolish after all.

Galileo Galilei was many things; a Catholic, a gifted mathematician and astronomer and a skilled debater. His sharp wit and acerbic tongue fitted in nicely with his natural ability for self-promotion. Not content with picking up on Copernicus's contentious theories, he also tackled what for some was a far greater beast; the ancient Greek wisdom of Aristotle. With his telescope and powerful presentations, Galileo was one part scientist, two parts circus show. The fact that Galileo couldn't even explain how the telescope actually worked, let alone why Jupiter's moons behaved as they did, gave his critics plenty of ammunition.

Still, the astronomer was not without supporters. Some – even those within the Church – grew to admire his presentations. He was, if nothing else, good value entertainment. While fellow academics in thrall to Aristotle refused to budge, the Church could not ever really fully condemn Galileo. For a man of his social standing there was no risk of ending up in any serious trouble.

Perhaps the reason why the Church allowed Galileo to continue to speak was due in part to an awareness on the part of the clergy that they were being used. Unable to silence him on their own patch, academics turned to the Church for back up. Science and the Church were not used to working in such a collaborative manner, and the relationship never really bloomed. In fact, back in 1611 Galileo's business trip to Rome had proved to be highly successful when he secured the endorsement of Jesuit astronomers.

1492 Christopher Columbus reaches America

1503 First African slaves taken to America

1572 St Bartholomew's Day Massacre

1577 – 1580 Francis Drake sails around world

Eventually, however, Galileo's opponents applied enough pressure for the Church to convene and give the matter some serious thought. Led by the Aristotelian academic Ludovico delle Colombe, Galileo was charged with heretical belief in theories that contradicted the Bible. Having suffered so severely at the hands of the Protestant reformers, Rome was not going to allow one of its own to challenge its authority so blatantly.

And so, sixteen years after the decree about Copernicus failed to put the matter to bed, Galileo Galilei stood in front of a Church Inquisition on charges of heresy because of his belief in that same theory. Galileo responded during the three-day hearing with typical wit and sarcasm, which, understandably, failed to win over many friends. In fact, the early support from the Jesuits went out the window and Galileo even managed to personally offend Pope Urban.

Unsurprisingly he was ordered to renounce his heretical opinions – stating clearly that he sincerely believed that the Earth did not move - and was sentenced to house arrest for his remaining years. Whether he did actually recant or not is of secondary importance. What matters more is that the Church managed to silence him. They would not be so fortunate in years to come.

If the Catholic Church was riled about Galileo it had less to do with the stars and telescopes than others might have thought. The issue was one of internal struggles over Biblical interpretation. Was Scripture to be viewed as immovable or could it be interpreted with a degree of flexibility? In the years to come these progressive versus traditional arguments would define the very nature of what it meant to be a Christian.

NEW HORIZONS

Marco Polo had already travelled east and returned to Venice with pockets full of jewels and a dozen stories for every shimmering gem. His journeys took place back in the final decades of the thirteenth century, but Europe would have to wait at least another hundred years before the world would open up again. The East became blocked by a rising Ottoman Empire and with the Black Death scything its way throughout Europe, travel slipped from the agenda.

The key was technology: specifically, ships. Once the Portuguese developed the sort that could cope with something a little wilder than the tame waters of the Mediterranean, the race began once more. The prospect of tapping into the lucrative trade in silk, gold, silver and spices was more than enough of an incentive.

The Portuguese set off first. Heading down the African coast they were able to establish trade routes with sub-Saharan Africa, bypassing the Islamic states in the north of the continent which had previously had a lock on an already flourishing slave and gold trading route. Eventually they made it back up to India and established further forts as they traded across towards Japan.

Christopher Columbus managed to stake a claim on North America for the Spanish, while in 1500 the Portuguese discovered land that would eventually become Brazil. To avoid an unseemly scrap between the two, the Pope intervened. This was in 1494 and the Treaty of Tordesillas split the world up between the two powers. The Portuguese got Africa, Asia and eastern South America while the Spanish received everything west of Brazil as well as the Pacific

1492
Christopher Columbus reaches America

1503
First African slaves taken to America

1572
St Bartholomew's Day Massacre

1577 – 1580
Francis Drake sails around world

Ocean islands. Later – much later – the Catholic Church would have to return to the region with its carving knife at the ready, but that's another story altogether.

There were other European powers with ambitions, and eventually Portugal would be overwhelmed by the sheer manpower of France, the Netherlands and England. But for now the plan was nice enough –the Portuguese and Spanish were allowed to divide up the land, its people and treasures between them.

At first both were a little disappointed. Their allotted territories failed to turn up anything like the riches of African gold. The Spanish pressed on inland. It was then that they changed their opinion. Among the Aztecs of Mexico and Incas of Peru they found civilisations as large as many back home. And thanks to the way that smallpox and other European diseases wiped out communities at a single stroke, the *conquistadors* had much of their killing taken care of. Of course, they still had to slaughter their way forward from time to time to take final control of the territories, but Central and South America gave up its treasures of gold and silver almost willingly.

To the North – where the Spanish had too few resources and too little interest – the French, Dutch and English began to settle, starting with the East coast. Of course, the Vikings had been there long before, but had never really amounted to much. Perhaps they had failed to bring enough diseases and muskets.

Gradually, as the Portuguese caved in to the others, the seeds of colonialism took root. While gold and silver had caught the eye of the explorers, the potential from crops of cotton, tobacco and sugar pointed to a long, sustainable future. And with the possibility of

1600 – 1614
East India Companies formed

1620
Mayflower leaves Plymouth

1618 – 1648
The Thirty Years' War

1754 – 1763
Anglo-French War, North America

slaves making up the labour force, Europe was hooked.

Slavery was, of course, nothing new. The African system had been in business long before the Spanish and Portuguese showed up with their guns, ammunition or other goods that caught the eye of local kings. Yet it was the sheer scale of the transatlantic slave trade that stands out. As many as 8 million died in transit, with a further 12 million lives lost either side of the transaction. It was only with the advance of genetic screening in the 2040s that any real degree of clarity about the numbers traded could be found. As many as 30 million Africans were taken across the Atlantic and put to work on the plantations – 1 person in every 3 from the continent.

HOW COULD THEY?

And what does all this have to do with the story of Christianity? Isn't this about science, technology, business or simply the highs and lows of global politics? It wasn't as if the Church was the main instigator of slavery, was it? Or does it matter that men and women of faith appeared to stand by, silent while all this was happening? Did they condone it, did they benefit from the horrors of slavery? Was Christianity to blame?

The truth is mixed. Early on in the Age of Exploration the conquistadors carried with them an assumed divine mandate to spread Catholicism throughout the world. For many it proved fatal. They abused their power and baptised indigenous people en masse without any attempt at making the process anything other than a banal formality. The incentive for the Europeans was even more base; some had been told that their men could not sleep with local heathens. Once baptised, however, they were fair game.

1492
Christopher Columbus reaches America

1503
First African slaves taken to America

1572
St Bartholomew's Day Massacre

1577 – 1580
Francis Drake sails around world

Tinkering with the broken machine, a new policy emerged in 1513; all conquistadors had to read aloud *the Requirement* – a statement that joined the dots between God's sovereignty, the power of the Church and the host country's new fate under threat of violence. Read out only in Latin or Spanish, the words themselves were little more than a sick joke.

While they might not have liked the method, there were plenty of Christians in Europe who believed in the authority of the Church to convert the world. Others were less able to airbrush the mistakes out, but voices speaking against the Church on this matter were left ignored. Even Pope Eugene IV's condemnation of slavery in the Canary Islands in the 1430s was swept aside.

Gradually the brutality of the early explorers was replaced with a more long-term view. The Catholic Church established missions within the new colonies. Of those, the most successful was the first Jesuit missionary Francisco de Xavier.

Arriving in Goa in May 1542, de Xavier travelled to southern India, spending three years working among pearl-fishers. From there he travelled to the East Indies and eventually Japan, dying before reaching China in 1552. A decade of travel towards the end of a life may not seem remarkable to modern readers, yet de Xavier's journey was among the most significant of the entire century. He worked with the zeal of the early Apostles, translating Scripture, educating children and praying for healing as he went. Baptisms were often large events, yet this was no attempt at arbitrary application of rules; the numbers were a reflection of de Xavier's genuine success at communicating the essence of Christianity to a people whose only

1600 – 1614
East India Companies formed

1618 – 1648
The Thirty Years' War

1620
Mayflower leaves Plymouth

1754 – 1763
Anglo-French War, North America

previous connection had been through the missionary journeys of the apostle Thomas in the first century.

Beatified by Pope Paul V in 1619, and canonised by Gregory XV in 1622, de Xavier's legacy was undeniably significant. The sheer number of schools alone that bear his name hint at his importance, yet had history swung in other directions the patron saint of missionaries could have found himself a more controversial, less celebrated figure. In Japan, de Xavier encouraged converts to destroy traditional temples and shrines, and his time in India did not pass without drama. His involvement in the Goa Inquisition – urging its creation in an attempt to punish those whose new found Christian faith had lapsed back towards Hinduism – made him a controversial figure. The allegations of torture made their way back home to Europe, where French philosopher Voltaire observed:

'Goa is sadly famous for its inquisition, which is contrary to humanity as much as to commerce. The Portuguese monks deluded us into believing that the Indian populace was worshiping The Devil, while it is they who served him.'

Then again, Voltaire was hardly Christianity's most ardent supporter.

EXIT

In North America the Catholic Church benefited from the ambitions of the French government. Dividing a large area up into Canada (to the east) and l'Acadie (to the west), the plan was to create a Catholic-only zone. It nearly worked, yet the British eventually got the upper hand.

1492
Christopher Columbus reaches America

1503
First African slaves taken to America

1572
St Bartholomew's Day Massacre

1577 – 1580
Francis Drake sails around world

Meanwhile, North America became a promised land for disaffected – and persecuted – European non-Catholics, particularly the Puritans pushed out by the Church of England. Their seventeenth-century Separatist movement was in need of a fresh start, and North America was the ideal location. Dutch and English, Puritan, Separatist, Baptist and Quaker; the east coast became home to the new pilgrims, hopeful of a better life.

And so we reach the end of an era. The world is about to get bigger. Not that this is anything new; from the moment that Moses led the Israelites away from the crashing waters and floating Egyptian corpses, the pursuit of God has been inextricably linked with physical journeys of discovery, risk and adventure. Did anyone know that that these journeys across the Atlantic would be the start of so much? They might not have known, but I suspect that they might have hoped.

Five hundred years after Christians began exporting their mixed motives across to the new world, one of their distant ancestors would write about the challenges of the struggle for survival. Eugene Peterson will be better known for far more than this simple comment, yet it seems fitting to insert it right now:

> As a pastor, I don't like being viewed as nice but insignificant. I bristle when a high-energy executive leaves the place of worship with the comment, 'This was wonderful, Pastor, but now we have to get back to the real world, don't we?' I had thought that we were in the most-real world, the world revealed as God's, a world believed to be in invaded by God's grace and turning on the pivot of Christ's crucifixion and resurrection…

1600 – 1614
East India Companies formed

1620
Mayflower leaves Plymouth

1618 – 1648
The Thirty Years' War

1754 – 1763
Anglo-French War, North America

> But America and suburbia and the ego compose my parish. Most of the individuals in this amalgam suppose that the goals they have for themselves and the goals God has for them are the same. It is the oldest religious mistake: refusing to countenance any real difference between God and us, imaging God to be a vague extrapolation of our desires, and then hiring a priest to manage the affairs between self and the extrapolation. And I, one of the priests they hired, am having none of it.
>
> Eugene H Peterson, *The Gift*

Peterson was right when he termed it the 'oldest religious mistake'. Some of those who travelled west from Europe were guilty in the extreme. Others avoided the trap. Somehow, centuries later, when the land had become a country, America would follow the same pattern, offering both the best and the worst of what it means to follow Christ, balancing contradiction for a season before withdrawing from the spotlight.

More than a comment on America, however, Peterson's words strike a chord worldwide; what precisely is the real world? Can the Church hope to compete with all those who claim to have found it far beyond its walls? For centuries the Church was by default the place where life's reality was discussed and defined. But not for long; a change was coming that would leave the Church struggling to relocate itself within a world turned upon its very head.

Chapter Eight

1492 – 1769
Ages of Reason and Awakenings

It really wasn't supposed to be this way. With Europe flexing its muscles east and west, bringing back tales of conquests and a steady flow of treasures, people were supposed to be feeling good. More importantly, the Church was meant to be coming out of all this with an altogether brighter halo. And why not? Finally Christianity was settling across the globe like Alpine snow. Shouldn't that be cause for even greater success back home?

The truth was rather different. The return of the missionaries and explorers introduced confusion rather than certainty to the waters. Instead of ignorance and gratitude they had encountered cultures (particularly in the east) that were highly advanced and with little need for the imposition of Christian values.

While France rose to become the dominant European superpower, the Church's political influence began to shift. Louis XIV ruled from 1643 to 1715 with a fully-developed God Complex – calling himself the 'Sun King' and declaring 'I am the state!' The Netherlands preferred tolerance to theological dogma and England – while not chasing Catholic terrorists intent on blowing up Parliament – drifted towards democracy.

As the Age of Exploration phased out, a new era began, one where the very fundamentals of life were questioned. Unlike the days of inquisitions and trials, Christianity now found itself on the receiving end of much of the questioning.

Rene Decartes was the man for the job. Being French helped, as did being a mathematician and a Catholic educated by Jesuits. Gradually Descartes developed a hypothesis; any statement considered to be true ought to be able to be proven as such. In other words,

1564
William Shakespeare born

1610
Galileo proves earth revolves around sun

1611
King James Bible

1641
Rene Descartes' *Meditations on First Philosophy*

reason was ranked above blind faith. Why should people be content with making mistakes, when the cold application of reason to any situation was bound to produce the better result?

Cartesianism took off. For many it was seen as a potential support to Christianity, yet as the buzz began to subside it became clear that Descartes' cold logic had a flaw in it. He had concluded famously that 'I think therefore I am', suggesting that thought itself was proof enough of his existence. As for God, well, since it was obvious that he could not have come up with so perfect and infinite a Divine Being, Descartes concluded that it must have been put there by God himself. It might seem odd today, but this simplistic 'What Human Could Have Created Such An Idea?' argument was supposed to convince others of God's existence.

It did not take long for the cracks to appear. In spite of Christian leaders adopting the rational approach as an attempt to reunify a divided Church, others began to apply reason to the idea of the Trinity. Could they find a rational explanation or a logical description? Of course not.

Throughout the seventeenth century, Christianity's influence was gradually eroded. Isaac Newton found that simple laws of physics could define the falling of an apple. Could they also be applied to the greater mysteries of life itself? His fellow Englishman, John Locke, took Cartesianism even further than its originator, drawing on the senses as the source of all information which he then subjected to the rigorous application of reason. Again, the Trinity didn't come out too well, yet Christianity itself was something he largely supported – so long as it was reasonable. God existed – Locke argued – but there was no need

1642 – 1651
English Civil War

1687
Isaac Newton's theory of gravity

1603
Peter the Great founds
St Petersburg

1748
Atlantic storm inspires
John Newton's *Amazing Grace*

to have him rule the country. Church and state should be separate and religious freedom protected. The Enlightenment was open for business.

For those who felt that the Trinity was tripped up by reason, Deism became a defining school of thought. The Bible's spiritual authority was questioned as its reputation as a distinctly human work grew. Much of what the Church held as evidence of God's intervention in life was labelled mere superstition. What mattered most was living a good, moral life.

While their arguments would be taken up by humanists and atheists in years to come, at the time English Deists were often held by those who saw themselves as potential refiners of the Church. They were merely carrying on where Luther left off; purging Christianity of superstitious nonsense. In France, however, Deists were less tolerant of the faith, as Voltaire made perfectly clear. Even on his deathbed Voltaire's wit and doubt were in tact, as, when asked to renounce the devil and finally turn to God he replied: 'Now is no time to be making new enemies.'

Deists were more than reactionaries in North America. Thomas Jefferson's crowning achievement of the Declaration of Independence – independence from the British Empire – resonates with his appreciation of the work of John Locke:

'We hold these truths to be self-evident, that all men are created equal, that they are endowed by their Creator with certain unalienable Rights, that among these are Life, Liberty and the pursuit of Happiness.'

The opening words underline Jefferson's faith in God, but do little to expand his approach to Christianity. For that, his book *The Life and Morals of Jesus of Nazareth* needs to be explored. Also known as the

1564
William Shakespeare born

1610
Galileo proves earth revolves around sun

1611
King James Bible

1641
Rene Descartes' *Meditations on First Philosophy*

Jefferson Bible, it contains a selective retelling of the life of Jesus, taken from the Gospels and presented in chronological order. However, it was what he left out that is noteworthy: starting with the birth of Christ there are no angels, genealogy, or prophecy. Later there are no miracles, no references to the Trinity and the divinity of Jesus, or any mention of Jesus' resurrection. Its final words betray the author's opinions clearly, drawing from John 19, but omitting anything that follows it:

> Now, in the place where he was crucified, there was a garden; and in the garden a new sepulchre, wherein was never man yet laid. There laid they Jesus. And rolled a great stone to the door of the sepulchre, and departed.

In Russia a history of anti-Catholic sentiment had fuelled the Orthodox Church, closing its ears to western ideas in much the same way that communism bolted its gates in the twentieth century. However, a few battles and a little political upheaval was all it took for Russia to find itself suddenly influence by external thought. When Russia assumed control of part of Ukraine in 1667, Catholicism crept in by the back door. A century and a half after Luther had started the process of Reform in the west, Nikon of Moscow began his own reformation of the Orthodox faith, trying to restore it to its original glories.

While the theory was nice enough, the reality was brutal. Many were resistant to change; Nikon's reforms were implemented with force, and thousands died. Famine and plague also took centre stage and by the time 1666 rolled in many Russians had given up all hope of life ever improving. Surely the antichrist was just around the

1642 – 1651
English Civil War

1687
Isaac Newton's theory of gravity

1603
Peter the Great founds
St Petersburg

1748
Atlantic storm inspires
John Newton's *Amazing Grace*

corner? Suicide suddenly seemed appealing.

With the Russian Orthodox Church split, the country needed a healer, a unifying figure who would draw the people together and soothe their collective pain. Instead they got Peter the Great. West was best for ol' Pete, and in his quest to absorb certain cultural trends from Europe he decided that beards were just a little too ancient and orthodox. So he had people shave theirs off, which many men did, keeping them in a box in case they should come in handy once they tried to get into heaven. He overtook the Church and used priests as informants if they heard of a treacherous activity among their flock. Poverty landed hard on those lower down the social order, and once more Russia was firmly embedded in a groove that would prove almost impossible to escape.

REVIVAL

Throughout the seventeenth and eighteenth centuries it became increasingly common for groups to look back to the early work that Luther carried out in reforming the Church and conclude that there was more yet to be done. As well as the Deists in England and France, history records a new group intent on completing the job: the Pietists. Taking their cue from a Lutheran pastor named Johann Arndt, the group saw Christianity in terms of the pursuit of a personal relationship with Christ. This meant that lifestyle was pushed high up on the agenda – higher than ritual, sacrament or any other Church-based activities. For some this was a dangerous heresy but for others it was a logical progression of the Reformation, as well as a vital reaction to the prevailing winds of revolution in England and struggles to the east.

The German-based movement embraced education as a key tool

1564
William Shakespeare born

1611
King James Bible

1610
Galileo proves earth revolves around sun

1641
Rene Descartes' *Meditations on First Philosophy*

for creating appropriate lifestyles. In Halle, near Leipzig, they founded a university as well as schools for younger pupils and training colleges for teachers. The aim was clear; society's reform would come through the classroom. It is not hard to imagine their optimism.

As the Pietists valued education, it was logical that they would favour mission as well. Of their many missionaries, the group known as the Moravians is perhaps the best known today. Thanks to their own renewal in the latter quarter of the twenty-first century their name today is synonymous with engagement with complex ethical and technological issues. It was not quite so back in the eighteenth century, but under the patronage of Nikolaus Ludwig von Zinzendorf und Pottendorf (himself a product of the university at Halle), a young believer named Christian David founded a community called Herrnhut – The Lord's Protection.

In an attempt to emulate the early Church, these Moravians prayed much, slept little, worked hard and avoided dancing, swearing and drunkenness. They were a hit. As numbers grew missionary groups were sent out to the Caribbean, North and South America, the Arctic, Africa, and the Far East. Often it was the unordained who travelled with the message, and they frequently evangelised to slaves. While their visibility remained questionable, their integration of social concern and religious devotion was a sign of things to come.

Remember Arminianism? It was the branch of Protestantism that rejected notions of predestination. Well, it was back in the news when a young preacher in Boston, Massachusetts took his place in the pulpit in 1731. For Jonathan Edwards, Arminianism had created a culture of apathy, a state where personal integrity was allowed to slip

1642 – 1651
English Civil War

1603
Peter the Great founds
St Petersburg

1687
Isaac Newton's theory of gravity

1748
Atlantic storm inspires
John Newton's *Amazing Grace*

simply because God's grace was sufficient. It was not enough to be called a Christian; you had to live it too.

That sermon – titled 'God Glorified in Man's Dependence' – called for a return to rigorous Calvinism. A little later his ideas broadened to include an emphasis on the need for a personal experience or encounter with God, and by the mid-1730s his Church numbers were up significantly.

What followed remains known as The First Great Awakening; a ramp up in the inexplicable presence of what could only be attributed to God's own activities. At the time it was called revival, reflecting the assumption that the Church had been in some kind of dormant state for years. The benefit of historical perspective questions the truth of such a claim.

What was beyond doubt, however, was the fact that Edwards was onto something remarkable. Ever since the British evangelist George Whitefield visited Edwards things had been getting increasingly intense. Conversions increased, and were generally accompanied by convulsions and a certain degree of hysteria. All the weeping and moaning in the seats confused many, but captivated even more.

Edwards did not have it easy all the time. His congregation turned against him around the same time that he started disciplinary proceedings in church against young people who had been reading beyond his list of authorised books. Yet he remained a figure of tremendous influence, particularly for those who returned to the question of what it meant to be human. As technology set the pace for debate throughout the twenty-first century, so Edwards' work was called upon as reference point. When it came to science and philos-

1564
William Shakespeare born

1610
Galileo proves earth revolves around sun

1611
King James Bible

1641
Rene Descartes' *Meditations on First Philosophy*

ophy Edwards was well read, and highly motivated. He chose to speak out about what he saw as a drift towards materialism, bringing the debate back to the role God plays as Creator behind all creation.

Whitfield's words went against the spirit of the Age of Enlightenment; rational thought was secondary to the whole-hearted devotion to God that was required of true believers. In England and North America he preached fire, brimstone and the essential connection with the emotions that he felt had been missing for far too long. The Moravians bought in on the whole package, as did a young Englishman named John Wesley and his brother Charles. Both had made their way to North American on board a ship sprinkled with Moravians – the kind of Christians who carried on with their study, prayer and work regardless of storms or squalls. The Wesleys were impressed, and by the time they landed were ripe for fresh instruction.

Both ended up following Whitfield, preaching to large crowds in fields across England. But with the Wesleys the heat was turned up; the crowds were larger, the convulsions were bolder and the cries were louder. Whitfied was less than happy about it all, yet the divisions that lay ahead applied to more than just these three. Calvin's doctrine of predestination became contentious; John and Charles Wesley were among those who rejected it as a misrepresentation of God who was defined by, among other things, grace. The Baptists, among others, were happy to continue in the other direction, many heading towards America's southern states.

With Charles Wesley's prolific hymn writing – as many as 10,000 in total – and John's oratorical skills, the brothers built more than a successful road show. They encouraged their – mainly Anglican –

1642 – 1651
English Civil War

1603
Peter the Great founds
St Petersburg

1687
Isaac Newton's theory of gravity

1748
Atlantic storm inspires
John Newton's *Amazing Grace*

listeners to pray together and unite in their attempts to achieve better standards of integrity and personal holiness.

John Wesley travelled constantly, more often than not on horseback, and often preaching two or three times a day. He was the archetypal prolific entrepreneur: helping the sick, investing in the Church and mobilising the help of the poor. Unlike others, however, he had no desire to become wealthy. Despite earning large sums from his publications (as much as £20,000 in total) he kept no more than £30 a year for himself – the typical wage of a worker. He rose in the small hours of each morning, worked constantly and died poor.

Perhaps he made a mistake when, aged forty-eight, he wed the widow, Mary Vazeille. After fifteen years of marriage she left him, and it is clear that the end of the relationship added to the self-doubt that had remained with him throughout his life. Aged sixty-three, he wrote to his brother: 'I do not love God. I never did. Therefore I never believed, in the Christian sense of the word. Therefore I am only an honest heathen ... And yet, to be so employed of God!'

Whatever the truth about Wesley's marriage and the impact of its ending, it appeared to have no seriously detrimental impact on his work. By the time he died aged eighty-seven (in 1791) he left behind a movement made up of 135,000 members and 541 itinerant preachers united under the name Methodist.

As he lay dying, with friends surrounding him, he repeated a simple mantra: 'Farewell, farewell.'

Finally, his breathing becoming ever heavier, he raised his arms and called out: 'The best of all is, God is with us. The best of all is, God is with us.'

Chapter Nine

1700 – 1851
The Change

Individuals rarely bring down entire nations single-handedly, particularly when they have been dead for sixty years. But John Law (1671–1729) came close.

Part gambler, part financier, part genius, part conman, Law was a Scottish entrepreneur who escaped from prison after killing a man in a duel about a girl. Once in France he hit upon an ingenious idea to raise much-needed finance for the French colony in Louisiana. According to Law, money was not real wealth; it was merely a tool to support trade. So he established a bank which issued its own bank notes. Printing more and more paper money, Law reaped astronomical rewards until, at the end of 1720, the bubble burst. Law did what he had done before and fled the country, although this time there were no second chances. He died impoverished and alone while the French middle classes, as well as the aristocracy, were ruined.

A couple of centuries later and Law's reputation would be renovated, but as France struggled through the eighteenth century, overburdened with debt and ruled by successive financially incompetent kings, Law's name remained mud.

Revolution was in the air. Technological innovation sparked the industrial revolution in the 1780s with the invention of steam engines, mechanised textile production and advances in iron production. The Americans resisted the imposition of taxes by the British, and within a decade had thrown off their colonial masters. So it was understandable that the French did not take kindly to Louis XVI's mismanagement of the economy. Thanks to his extravagant tastes bankruptcy was imminent. His calls for increased taxes failed to impress, and on 14 July 1789 a mob stormed the Bastille prison in

1757
Pope allows non-Latin Bibles

1776
US Declaration of Independence

1788
First British convicts to Australia

1789
Bastille stormed, French Revolution begins

central Paris – a key symbol of royal tyranny. The French Revolution had begun.

What followed was brutal and barbaric, despite the fact that the early days were infused with a sense of righteous triumph. Finally the ideals of the Enlightenment were being put to work, tearing down the excesses of the past and lifting up the common man. The American model served as a compass for the revolutionaries, who drafted a Declaration of the Rights of Man which allowed the King to remain in position, although without retaining any real power to speak of. Yet gradually the revolution drifted off course. In 1792 the king was dethroned, and the following January he was beheaded, quickly followed by his wife, Marie Antoinette. Within a year chaos ruled, and the days had a new name: the reign of terror.

Across France guillotines were set up and thousands were beheaded. Aristocrats were first up the steps, but commoners suspected of treason were soon following them. It was only with the death of the revolutionaries' leader – Robespierre – in 1794 that the terror began to ease slightly, easing still further when, in 1796 a young general named Napoleon began asserting his military might in the south. Whatever hint there had been of democracy went the same way as the aristocrats and traitors as Napoleon launched an audacious campaign to extend his power in Europe.

What all this has to do with Christianity is simple. The Enlightenment had shown a new way to be human. Old systems of power and control were rejected and turfed out in favour of the dependable logic of reason and the power of the common man. While the Reformation had played a clear part in the formation of

1814
George Stephenson's first railway steam train

1815
Napoleon defeated at Waterloo

1833
British pass Slavery Abolition Act

1840 – 1842
Britain and China's Opium Wars

such ideals – rooting out superstition and promoting the value of the individual – Christianity in general was often seen as part of the problem that needed purging.

Revolutionary France was not a good place to be for those who professed faith in Christ. As the Reign of Terror attempted to unshackle the country from the irons of religion, they channelled the likes of Nero and Diocletian. Some of their measures were petty – removing bells from church towers and 'Saint' from street names. Other methods were cruel; forcing a little under 10,000 priests to marry and resign, with 30,000 others made to leave France. The guillotine took her share of the most obstinate, while many Catholics made their way to French Quebec and the relative safety of British rule that was more tolerant of religion.

Despite the attempts to secularise France and turn any remaining spiritual urges over to the new state-sanctioned religion – the Cult of the Supreme Being – Robespierre's attempts failed. Created from nothing more than thin air and a desire to retain control, the Cult of the Supreme Being was a little flimsy on detail. There was no god, but the eponymous Supreme Being who quite liked France and who preferred it when people were linked by his 'boundless chain of love and happiness'. The calendar was tinkered with (ten-day weeks and festival days in celebration of Reason, Hard Work and Virtue) but, apart from the introduction of the metric system of measurement, none of the madness remained. Why? Because Napoleon understood that the Catholic Church was an effective tool for maintaining social order. He struck a deal with Rome which allowed him to keep the Church property seized by the Revolution, at the same time as re-

1757
Pope allows non-Latin Bibles

1776
US Declaration of Independence

1788
First British convicts to Australia

1789
Bastille stormed, French Revolution begins

establishing Catholicism as the country's primary – if somewhat neutered - religion.

Something had changed. Within just a handful of years the landscape had shifted entirely. Christianity had gone from being an inspiration to a pariah to a muted lackey of a power-obsessed ruler. None of these identities were new to the Church, but the speed of the costume changes was bewildering to say the least. For anyone observing it was clear that the great faith might not be carved in stone after all.

THE NEXT STEPS

So, what follows is the death of religion, right? We enter a period of rapid decline, wholesale transformation and emerge into the light with a religion-free world a little like that picture by Robespierre but without so much of the crazy stuff. Isn't that the way things developed from here?

Of course not. The seeds that were sown by – among others – the French Revolution took far longer to germinate. The fact was that in the immediate aftermath of the days of guillotines and Temples of Reason, Christianity experienced one of its most effective periods ever. It had happened before (and you don't have to flick too far into this book to find plenty of examples) and it would happen again. The twenty-first century would be particularly marked out by this, with atheism appearing to rise up against and overpower the foolish faithful ones. Yet the fireworks and the smoke would lead to nothing as, like post-revolutionary France, the cycle of faith and unbelief followed well-worn grooves.

The nineteenth century saw a renewal of interest in the Catholic

1814
George Stephenson's first railway steam train

1815
Napoleon defeated at Waterloo

1833
British pass Slavery Abolition Act

1840 – 1842
Britain and China's Opium Wars

Church throughout Europe, with France returning to a modified system that limited the Pope's power, authority and status. But it was in America that the horizons were initially the brightest.

The Great Awakening had given birth to Methodism and drawn back the curtains on a faith marked by personal integrity and emotional connection, yet in England it had died down by the latter half of the eighteenth century. Not so in North America, though. The revivals continued, following the settlers as they headed west, and Methodist and Baptist churches flourished, particularly in the South.

Southern ways headed north, with the camp meeting format being borrowed by lawyer turned Presbyterian minister, Charles Finney. New York state and city both swayed in hired halls as Finney preached a message that urged his listeners to exercise free will and repent, as well as to accept God's grace-laden forgiveness. Works were not essential to salvation, but were a clear sign of the faith of the individual. The message went down well and helped nurture the sense that social transformation might be related to spiritual growth.

These days were ripe with opportunity and interest in God. Joseph Smith, confused by the revival meetings in New York State, asked God to clear things up. Apparently God told him that none of the current crop of Churches was on the right track and that he should await further orders. Years later, and thanks to an angel named Moroni, Mormonism was alive and well. The Church of Latter-day Saints signed people up to a faith that started with conventional Christianity and added such treats as polygamy, multiple levels of heaven and the possibility of baptism for the dead. The message went

1757
Pope allows
non-Latin Bibles

1776
US Declaration of Independence

1788
First British convicts to
Australia

1789
Bastille stormed, French
Revolution begins

down well, which – depending on how you see things – is either a compliment to Smith's power as a salesmen or evidence of the enduring gullibility of the everyday person. I suppose it could be because Smith was right all along, although the sect's decline and eventual drift towards the fringes of anonymity over the coming centuries might suggest otherwise.

A little more successful was Baptist minister, William Miller. His Seventh-day Adventist Church – as it eventually became – was both highly organised and considerably less controversial than Smith's Church of Latter-day Saints. However, Miller did flirt with the ridiculous, claiming that the return of Christ was absolutely certain to occur at some point during the year 1843. He did at least have the good grace to, in 1844, admit that he had been wrong, although not before he commented that he did 'still believe that the day of the Lord is near, even at the door'. Little wonder that the incident became known as the Great Disappointment.

There was genuine cause for optimism with the Church, in spite of the errors of the above. Having evangelised the slaves for the better part of a century, it was time for a shift in Christianity. The old arguments in favour of slavery gradually lost their grip as the Christian opposition spread from the fringes in towards the centre. While the Quakers and Mennonites were vocal opponents in the previous century, eventually joined by the Baptists and Methodists, it was not until 1807 that the much-needed change began to emerge. On 25 March the British Parliament passed the Slave Trade Act, abolishing the trade in slaves throughout the then rather sizeable British Empire. The campaign was led by William Wilberforce (a

1814
George Stephenson's first railway steam train

1815
Napoleon defeated at Waterloo

1833
British pass Slavery Abolition Act

1840 – 1842
Britain and China's Opium Wars

Christian politician and founder of the Church Mission Society) and influenced largely by Olaudah Equiano, an ex-slave turned author and anti-slavery campaigner. Together they managed to combine faith and politics to produce a righteous outcome.

Yet it was not enough. The Industrial Revolution was lining the pockets of those wealthy enough to be able to afford the tools and the factories, but for the poor souls who had migrated from the country to the cities in order to work among the cogs and the coal smoke, life was pretty terrible. Overcrowding, poor sanitation, lack of education and crushing poverty combined to make life unacceptable for external observers. Friedrich Engels was outraged enough to trash the ruling classes in his 1845 work *Condition of the Working Class of England*, and eventually play a key role in the formation of communism.

Equally life-changing was the birth of Victorian social activism. One part evangelism, one part social concern, the renegade believers flew in the face of Anglican disinterest and took the gospel into the congested heart of the slums.

The results were significant thanks to the work of groups like the freshly created Salvation Army – founded by Methodist breakaway William Booth in the 1860s. Booth endured the ridicule for the uniforms and quasi-military approach to inner city mission, but there was no doubting his impact. Drug addicts, prostitutes and alcoholics were 'General' Booth's first targets. These undesirables of society had been comprehensively overlooked, and Booth provided them with employment and an explanation of the need to follow Christ.

Booth was not alone. Thomas Barnardo established homes for

1757
Pope allows non-Latin Bibles

1776
US Declaration of Independence

1788
First British convicts to Australia

1789
Bastille stormed, French Revolution begins

thousands of orphaned children while Lord Shaftesbury founded the Ragged Schools Union and provided the children trapped in poverty with a sound education. Shaftesbury also pushed for legal reform to benefit those working in factories and mines, while in Parliament he was joined by William Gladstone, the eventual Prime Minister. His concern for social reform led him to tackle what he saw as social ills – in particular drink and prostitution. The temperance movement grew as a result, with not only British but continental European and American evangelicals urging others to give up alcohol in favour of good Christian living.

Whole communities in industrial cities sprang up thanks to the work of philanthropists intent on using their wealth to create pockets of utopia based on Christian ideals. Chocolate magnates George and Richard Cadbury happened to be Quakers, and like Sir Titus Salt in the 1850s, built houses, schools, hospitals, parks and leisure facilities for their workers.

This was a move pioneered – and powered – by largely English speaking evangelicals, yet it would be wrong to apportion all credit to the British. Social reformers were at work in pockets across Europe, and in spite of the errors of the attempted Orthodox reform, the Church in Russia enjoyed something of a boom.

Already impacted by the advances of the Industrial Revolution – and some time before the chaos of their own political one – Russians were increasing in number. The introduction of elders (*startsy*) brought with them a focal point for Christians to be drawn to. Frequently monastic in their approach to life, nevertheless these men showed just what it meant to reconnect with the roots of Christian

1814
George Stephenson's first railway steam train

1815
Napoleon defeated at Waterloo

1833
British pass Slavery Abolition Act

1840 – 1842
Britain and China's Opium Wars

spirituality. Others headed off to the east, reaching the very edge of the Russian lands, hopping in boats and evangelising to islanders of the north Pacific. Some made their way to Alaska, creating an affection for the Russian Orthodox Church there that remains to this day.

Not everybody embraced the ideas of social reform. German philosopher Immanuel Kant had earlier questioned the use of Enlightenment-era rational thought to analyse God. Instead he suggested that reason only goes so far; God himself is surely beyond such physical measurement? The progression of his logic brought him to a point of doubting God's very existence and falling back upon the 'I just need to live a good life' argument.

Kant's idea struck a chord. Others developed his ideas, adding in (as Jean-Jacques Rousseau did) that humans were essentially happy until things like civilisation came along and messed it up. The 'noble savage' introduced the idea that not only should we be pursuing a reconnection with nature, but that the world itself was perfectly well left alone. Thus Victorian Romanticism retreated to its bedroom and refused to come out.

Like all teenagers, the Victorian Romantics dredged up cultural artefacts from the distant past and heralded them as new, authentic and to die for. Particular favourites were the days before the Age of Reason, with their knights, maidens and epic tales of honour and virtue. The art, music, poetry and prose that emerged was truly great (think Goya and Turner, Beethoven and Wagner, Byron, Shelley and Keats and Edgar Allen Poe and Washington Irving).

It wasn't all exotic drugs and long wanderings across windswept

1757
Pope allows non-Latin Bibles

1776
US Declaration of Independence

1788
First British convicts to Australia

1789
Bastille stormed, French Revolution begins

hills in search of enlightenment. Theology during the time was shaped in particular by the likes of Danish philosopher and theologian Søren Kierkegaard.

Writing in his journal just three years before his death, he got to the heart of the matter of what was wrong with the Church:

> I ask: what does it mean when we continue to behave as though all were as it should be, calling ourselves Christians according to the New Testament, when the ideals of the New Testament have gone out of life? The tremendous disproportion which this state of affairs represents has, moreover, been perceived by many. They like to give it this turn: the human race has outgrown Christianity.

Kierkegaard took Kant's ideas of God being beyond reason and turned them further back in towards the individual. It was personal choice, personal integrity that mattered, not hollow bleatings in large buildings celebrating state-sanctioned religion. After all, 'a religious movement must be served religiously - otherwise it is a sham!' (Journals, 1851).

To modern readers, Kierkegaard's words are familiar – particularly for those Christian readers among us. Yet in the century after his death, the Dane's name was held hostage by those marching under the various flags of postmodernism. They ignored his theology and focussed instead on his pronouncements on individualism. Eventually they would lose the battle and release him back to the Church from which his ideas came.

1814
George Stephenson's first railway steam train

1815
Napoleon defeated at Waterloo

1833
British pass Slavery Abolition Act

1840 – 1842
Britain and China's Opium Wars

THE CRISIS

With theology pushing personal integrity and social activists meeting the needs of society's outcasts, you could be forgiven for thinking that the Church was in a pretty good state. In some ways it was – the legacies of the above remain today – yet for some reason it was grossly ill-equipped to deal with what came next.

Science turned against religion. We have seen already how it was used to uphold belief in God, but by the time the nineteenth century settled in, there was less need for God to be tacked on to whatever discoveries were making the news. Secularism was gradually shifting from the margins towards the centre of debate, and some elements of the Church flew into a panic. Darwin's theory of natural selection caught those who had accepted a literal translation of the Bible off guard.

Some responded by taking a fresh look at the bible. Liberal Christianity evolved with the argument that the Old Testament might be more fiction than fact. Like Jefferson and the other Deists before, liberal theologians happily ignored the miracles of the New Testament. Science sat easily with theology for those who were able to take Christianity as an experience of God, through faith in Christ, in community with others. In the USA a fresh movement known as modernism grew from this viewpoint, and for perhaps the first time in its history, Christianity found itself not being merely accepted or rejected by a culture, but radically reinterpreted by it.

Although it may appear that those on the liberal wing were drifting off on their own, they remained connected with the aims of the social activists that had been born out of the evangelical wing of

1757
Pope allows non-Latin Bibles

1776
US Declaration of Independence

1788
First British convicts to Australia

1789
Bastille stormed, French Revolution begins

the Church. While they might not have agreed how they came to be there in the first place, the points of common ground were that there was little value in talking exclusively about life after death when there were millions uneducated, starving and outcast among us.

Not everyone was happy, though. Many went through this Crisis of Faith with a new, liberal enemy lined up in their sights. Others – like the Roman Catholic Church – experienced what could be described less as a crisis and more as a period of denial. Pope Pius IX declared that he was infallible and that liberalism was wrong. End of story.

This formal declaration of Papal infallibility was a little contentious at the time, with some members leaving the Church as a result. Others kept quiet, but over time the opposition would grow, eventually putting considerable pressure on the Vatican to admit that there was ample evidence to refute the papal claim.

If Pius IX leant towards the Church for support, many evangelicals looked to Scripture for refuge. How could liberalism be right, they argued, when the Bible was God's own handbook for life? It was infallible and utterly in opposition to science itself. The case, many believed was closed.

TODAY

Perspective does funny things to history. I'm tempted to see the social action of these days as one of the high points of the Christian story. What could be better than these days of God-sparked revolution and social change? Only the time of the early Church comes close, when subversion took on a different form, yet, I suppose, with similar

1814
George Stephenson's first railway steam train

1815
Napoleon defeated at Waterloo

1833
British pass Slavery Abolition Act

1840 – 1842
Britain and China's Opium Wars

results.

Why does all this appeal so much? It's the contrast with today. Where many in the Church are choking on fear and living life as small and as well-camouflaged as they possibly can, the social reformers – much like the martyrs that came before them – had none of it. Theirs was a faith painted in blood; ours seems to be wearing rags by comparison.

It's tempting to believe this, but I cannot sell myself over to it fully. Why? Because if this search for the story is teaching us anything it is that the threads of the very best of Christianity weave throughout the whole of history. In every century – and, I'm guessing every year and month and day too – there are the signs of us at our best.

And our worst.

Chapter Ten

1850 – 1944
The Speed of Change

If the Church had experienced any success in the nineteenth century – and there is plenty of fuel for both sides of the argument – the first five decades that followed left it bloodied, defeated and ignored at the side of the road. What had taken centuries to build – and generations to begin to understand – was seemingly wiped out almost overnight. This was the dawn of not one but many new eras; the modern, the postmodern, the global and the all-but-totally-annihilated. Many Christians had coped well enough when the greatest challenges they faced came in discreet, easily defined boxes labelled 'Science' and 'Poverty'. But with the dawn of the twentieth century those boxes were multiplied many, many times. Confused? You bet they were.

For the best part of the nineteenth century, Christians had been taking their message out to the rest of the world. It was the century of African, Asian and South Pacific missions, many carried out by independent and non denominational societies like the Church Mission Society, the Baptist Missionary Society and the Netherlands Missionary Society. The singular lack of creativity when it comes to the names hints at their single-minded focus. At their best, the missionaries to Africa brought freedom and fresh hope to a land that had been systematically robbed and raped from within and without since the Age of Exploration. Liberated slaves from Europe and the USA were supported by thriving missions and Christianity spread as indigenous people were finally given freedom to explore the faith for themselves. Hudson Taylor and other missionaries to China provided much-needed medical and educational support that went down particularly well among those at the wrong end of the social scale. Japanese Christians, after a slow start, soon emerged in great

1861 – 1865
American Civil War

1859
Charles Darwin's
On the Origin of Species

1867
Karl Marx's *Das Kapital*

1882
Friedrich Nietzsche announces
'God is dead'

numbers, thanks to the non-partisan work of Dutch Reformed, Catholic and Presbyterian missionaries.

At their not-so-best, Christians were guilty of fostering an insular mindset that would prove a source of great injustice in years to come. The Dutch Calvinists, known as the Boers, nurtured racial divisions that bred the infamous apartheid system that blighted South African life for much of the second half of the twentieth century. In Australia the Church was too often silent – and sometimes complicit – in the many abuses handed down to the indigenous people. In India, the Church ended up on the wrong side of the political divide, eventually forced into the role of observer as a diminutive Hindu man delivered one of the most remarkable displays of Christ-like leadership ever seen.

MEANWHILE...

The missionaries had long before finished with North America, yet America itself was far from finished. The Civil War pitched north against south, and the geographical divisions were mirrored by the opposition between denominations. The south was home to a greater sense of cohesion than the north; while immigration had brought Catholic, Lutheran, Reformed and Orthodox to the eastern seaboard, the South remained a largely Methodist and Protestant zone. During the fighting between 1861 and 1865, both sides claimed God's mandate; Churches in the south heralded their preservation of old-time values while those in the north were convinced that the battle was their divinely appointed mission to purge society of a great evil.

When the smoke cleared the hoped-for harmony failed to appear. The south – humiliated, impoverished and full of resentment –

1906 – 1909
Asuza Street Revival, USA

1914 – 1919
First World War

1938
Kristallnacht, Germany

1939 – 1945
Second World War

asserted its independence with a growing sense of unique identity. The idea that the country – and opinion – could be systematically reconstructed was treated as a joke and as cultures clashed, rebellions emerged. The Jim Crow laws – apartheid by any other name – allowed for social divisions between black and white to continue, while the emergence of numerous groups of white supremacists (most famously the Ku Klux Klan) aligned nominal Christianity with hatred, violence and murder. From 1882 to 1968 a colossal 4,743 people were lynched; murdered often in front of a jeering, cheering public. Of those victims, 3,446 were black.

Hatred did not have a complete stranglehold, however. The south was home to the emerging holiness movement which flowed from the eighteenth-century revivals. At its core was the belief that two conversions were needed: the first dealing with the repentance of sin, and the second providing 'sanctification' – being made right with God, with a holy life following. There was much disagreement about how such sanctification could be defined, yet in spite of the numerous different congregations that flowed out of it, the holiness movement invigorated the Church with a dedication to integrity and passion. To outsiders it all looked a little odd, however.

The most profound impact of the holiness movement was the formation of Pentecostalism. People still argue over who should earn the title of Father to the movement, and opinion generally falls between one of two men; a one-eyed black son of former slaves or a white preacher accused of sodomy, who praised the Ku Klux Klan and went off on a final voyage in search of the Ark of the Covenant and Noah's Ark. William Seymour (he of the limited eyesight) was a

1861 – 1865
American Civil War

1859
Charles Darwin's
On the Origin of Species

1867
Karl Marx's *Das Kapital*

1882
Friedrich Nietzsche announces
'God is dead'

remarkable man who was solely devoted to experiencing a more profound personal revelation of God. He would wander around the packed hall on Azusa Street in downtown Los Angeles in 1906 with dollar bills falling out of his pockets. The notes had been placed there by those attending the meeting, for Seymour had little time for taking collections or worrying about money. Instead, his satisfaction was derived from the sight of people from every race in the city gathering to encounter the Holy Spirit in much the same way that the members of the early Church had done on the very first Pentecost.

Charles Parham (the one with the scandal attached to him) was a more complex fellow. While Seymour – his one-time pupil – was perhaps guilty of being naïve in his assumptions that people would put aside their personal agendas and join him in pursuit of God, Parham was calculating and logical. He knew enough about human nature to help establish Pentecostalism in its infancy. Like all salesmen, Parham was keen on building something that would stand out, and it was perhaps due to this difference in the two men that they fell out.

The Pentecostal movement grew rapidly. Seymour may have not held ambitions for a denomination to follow, but others were less humble. Splintering like dried wood under a blunt axe, the Pentecostal movement spread across the globe. Perhaps these splits helped propel the message, for, within a century, Pentecostalism would find itself one of the largest – and most rapidly growing – elements within the Church. A congregation of 600 million and rising was nothing to be sniffed at in those days.

One final point. This might seem like an odd time to flick back to the days of the twelfth century mystics, but it's worth a trip.

1906 – 1909
Asuza Street Revival, USA

1914 – 1919
First World War

1938
Kristallnacht, Germany

1939 – 1945
Second World War

Joachim of Fiore was just such a man, the sort who took a pilgrimage from his native Sicily to the Holy Land and returned by way of a seven-year period of self-imposed seclusion as a hermit. At the time his was an internationally recognized name, largely for his teachings on what he saw as the three ages to Creation's history. As he saw it, the 'Eternal Gospel' was divided thus: the Age of the Father, the Age of the Son and the Age of the Holy Spirit.

He was well known and revered. Rumour has it that Richard the Lionheart wanted to stop by on his way to slaughtering the Turks, but the diaries just couldn't fit together. Eventually, the passing of time carried away his reputation as a man with a gift for insight, leaving Joachim of Fiore as just another of history's footnotes.

Until Azusa.

They might not have known it then, but the first Pentecostals were embarking upon a journey that would eventually rekindle the words of the ancient mystic. In time, the notion of the Eternal Gospel would be cited by many as further evidence that the events of 1906 were more than an overly-enthusiastic collection of overseas visitors.

According to Joachim of Fiore, the Age of God the Father ran parallel to the Old Testament. It ended with the death and resurrection of Christ, ushering in the next two-thousand year period of God the Son. Gradually it became common to claim that the unprecedented events in the less glamorous corners of Los Angeles in 1906 marked the clear transition into the Age of the Holy Spirit.

As The Great Emergence unfurled itself a century later, for some the picture pulled a little more sharply into focus. Azusa marked a transition, but to what? Was this the beginning of the end, or simply

1861 – 1865
American Civil War

1867
Karl Marx's *Das Kapital*

1859
Charles Darwin's
On the Origin of Species

1882
Friedrich Nietzsche announces
'God is dead'

the third of a five act play? And if this really did mark the start of God revealing himself primarily through the Holy Spirit, just how bold and varied a palette would he be painting with?

DEATH

But those questions were a long way off. At the start of the twentieth century the world was poised for something great. In spite of what was happening in the colonies or the halls of downtown Los Angeles, God was in trouble, or so one man thought.

'God is dead.' Friedrich Nietzsche could not have put it any more clearly. Advances in science had – according to the German/Polish philosopher – brought society to the point of rendering God obsolete. This was quite a change for the man who, aged twenty had written a poem to 'The Unknown God'. In it he claimed: 'I want to know you - even to serve you.'

Raised as a Lutheran, Nietzsche rebelled against the artificiality of the world around him. How could Christians be so *weak*? How could they hide from the realities of the world around them – the changes, the shifts, the transformation that was so clearly visible to anyone who dared open their eyes? Like Kierkegaard, he approached the bedside of Christianity and found that the patient was dangerously weak.

How different would it have been if Nietzsche had not fully abandoned the faith of his youth? It is impossible to tell. Would the insanity that descended upon him during his final years have been avoided? None can say. Yet surely there is a chance that the Church might have listened a little more carefully had his words not been dipped in such poison. If the Church had learned to stand up and

1906 – 1909
Asuza Street Revival, USA

1914 – 1919
First World War

1938
Kristallnacht, Germany

1939 – 1945
Second World War

fight the words that accused Christ of such weakness – as well as owning up to their own hypocrisy and self-interest – perhaps the years that followed might have been different.

Yet the reaction to Nietzsche's attacks on Christianity were nothing like this idealistic picture. Evangelicals closed their ears and eyes to the criticisms. Borrowing the morals of the Victorian Christian activists, but conveniently forgetting their devotion to self-sacrificial help of those rejected by society, in the USA many Christians pinned their hopes on prohibition. If only they could cut down the amount of booze that people were hurling down their throats, then surely everything would be ok? The ridiculous notion of such insularity may be amusing today, yet it was a tragic mistake at the time.

The liberal wing of the Church adopted a different approach. They became concerned with social reform rather than personal salvation, and overseas mission rose up the agenda. Nowhere was there enough support for those few voices who decried the descent into chaos and genocide.

With twenty per cent of the world's Jewish population living in Russia at the end of the nineteenth century, the ascent of Alexander III to the throne was problematic. The Jews were an easy target for anyone willing to stir up nationalism, and the Tsar encouraged a series of pogroms – or anti-semitic riots – throughout his thirteen-year reign. The trigger for these pogroms was the assassination of Tsar Alexander II, for which some blamed the Jewish population. With increasing efficiency, until, in 1905, as many as 2,500 Jews were killed during riots in Odessa. The Russian Orthodox Church offered no opposition to the pogroms. Instead it blamed the Jews for the misery

1861 – 1865
American Civil War

1867
Karl Marx's *Das Kapital*

1859
Charles Darwin's
On the Origin of Species

1882
Friedrich Nietzsche announces
'God is dead'

endured by Russian peasants. A million Jews fled Russia, heading west to the apparent safety of Europe. Anti-semitism followed them though, and their position remained dangerously unsafe.

As the First World War erupted, the French, British and Russians suspected that the fighting would be over quickly. Whether the Germans and Austro-Hungarians agreed is another matter, but four years later, in 1918, there was no ambiguity about what had just occurred. 60 million soldiers had been mobilised, and only 40 million had returned home. Fearful of revolt by their two million Armenian Christians, the Ottoman Empire slaughtered as many as half of them, and forced the rest to either leave or convert to Islam.

It was a war to end all wars: the Great War, the like of which would never be seen again. A generation of men returned home, traumatised by what they had seen, yet unable (not just unwilling) to describe it. Humanity had sunk lower than any could have previously imagined. God? There was no sign of intervention. Perhaps Nietzsche was right after all. Certainly the Church seemed silent on the matter.

The generation that grew up with fathers buried in some foreign field or lost to the nightmares that raged through the darkness, witnessed rapid changes. Russia revolted and embraced communism, rejecting God entirely in the process. Germany, struggling with debt and defeat, ran towards nationalism, embracing Adolf Hitler's adaptation of Nietzsche's thoughts on the value of strength over weakness.

The Church was not wholly irrelevant, however. For Hitler, the seal of approval from the clergy was an important stepping stone. In 1933 the German Christians were victorious in elections within the Protestant Church, and made few enemies – other than their victims

1906 – 1909
Asuza Street Revival, USA

1914 – 1919
First World War

1938
Kristallnacht, Germany

1939 – 1945
Second World War

– when they denied baptism to Jews and forbade marriage between Christian and Jew.

Some opposed. Martin Niemoller, a Lutheran, gathered support and created the Confessing Church. One of their leaders, Karl Barth, attacked the fascists with a Reformation-continuing argument that dragged the Church back towards the person of Jesus Christ. God's truth – and our example – was revealed perfectly through his Son alone. There was no room for manipulative theology that tried to justify anti-Semitism by claiming that in nature God reveals an affection for the survival of the fittest. That, Barth argued, was simply not Christ-like.

Hitler's efficiency was astounding. Not only did he want to purge society of Jews, he wanted to record quite how thoroughly he did it. The Nazi records of exterminations became contentious documents, valued by those in search of the truth about their distant relatives, denied by others who wished to revise the history of the Holocaust.

But what of the Church during the Second World War? The rise of the Brown Christians – clergy who supported the Nazis – proved controversial. Debates about the extent to which they were coerced continued long after their death, yet by the time that Hitler was at war with the rest of the world, the support of the Church meant little to him.

Its opposition, however, very nearly changed the course of history. Before the war Pope Pius XI decried Nazism and urged his bishops to tear it down during their sermons. Yet it was not enough, and his death on the eve of the war robbed many of a focal point of opposition. His replacement – Pope Pius XII – adopted a different approach. Knowing he was essentially powerless, Pius XII chose to

1861 – 1865
American Civil War

1867
Karl Marx's *Das Kapital*

1859
Charles Darwin's
On the Origin of Species

1882
Friedrich Nietzsche announces
'God is dead'

ignore much of what was going on under Hitler's reign. He was supportive of the Fuhrer, feigning deafness and opposing Nazism as weakly as he could.

Dietrich Bonhoeffer, however, was far less ambiguous. The German theologian, like Karl Barth who was frustrated by liberal theology, felt that by minimising the authority of Scripture the liberal approach had robbed the Church of much of its relevance. As those were times for a relevant Church, Bonhoeffer chose to act. He travelled to India to study non-violent resistance with Gandhi and returned to Germany. There, as part of the Confessing Church, he opposed Nazism and, in 1939, joined with high-ranking military officers in planning to kill Hitler. It was not until 1944 that those plans were ready to be put into action, yet the July 20 Plot failed when all those years of planning were frustrated by the simple act of someone moving the suitcase containing the bomb out of Hitler's range.

Bonhoeffer's execution was brutal. Stripped, tortured and led naked into the execution yard, he was hoisted by meathooks to a noose formed by piano wire. It took half an hour for him to die. A month later the Nazis surrendered.

THE QUESTIONS

Where had God been throughout the war? Where, for that matter, had the Church been? The period of questioning lasted long into the night. There were no easy answers, and sacrifice had been borne by so many millions of soldiers and innocent civilians on both sides of the war. There was little point in apportioning blame.

1906 – 1909
Asuza Street Revival, USA

1914 – 1919
First World War

1938
Kristallnacht, Germany

1939 – 1945
Second World War

Or was there? Slowly, ever so slowly, society would begin to face questions that would previously have been unthinkable. Anti-Semitism was a reality, one that needed to be admitted and confessed to. The Church had been silent for too long, fussing about alcohol while racism and fascism marched on unchecked. Christians had been struggling to keep up with the changes in the world ever since science began to assert its independence, and now those who claimed to value the fundamentals above everything else appeared at best wholly out of touch and at worst cruel, ignorant and distinctly ungodly.

Liberalism had failed too; where was the moral compass when it was needed? There was little appetite for the social gospel any more, as it was all that any country could do to rebuild after such a loss of life.

The Church, by and large, had failed. A generation of young men and women had seen it first hand, and now, so had their children. A colossal challenge was facing Christianity; would its followers find the answers to the whole new set of questions that were about to be asked by a culture for whom Church was rapidly becoming irrelevant?

There can be little wonder at what happened next. The horror of humanity's worst acts could not simply be switched off, any more than the sense of God's distance could be bridged. But did the Church have no option other than to sit quietly on the floor by the altar as an endless stream of turned backs shuffled out of the door? Was there no option other than resignation? Could it only observe?

Chapter Eleven

1950 – 1983
Rebuilding

On the subject of Jewish identity:

> Moreover, they are nothing but thieves and robbers who daily eat no morsel and wear no thread of clothing which they have not stolen and pilfered from us by means of their accursed usury. Thus they live from day to day, together with wife and child, by theft and robbery, as archthieves and robbers, in the most impenitent security.

The words come from before the war, which in itself is of no real surprise. What should concern us is the identity of the man who wrote such vitriolic phrases. His name was Martin Luther, and these lines are in no way unique. On many different occasions the father of the Reformation went out of his way to target the Jews. He suggested burning their synagogues and schools, destroying houses and prayer books and withdrawing all form of protection offered other citizens as they travelled.

To call this puzzling runs the risk of appearing flippant in the light of the appalling atrocities of the Holocaust. Yet there are questions that need to be asked today, just as the Church faced a much-needed period of self-reflection after the camps were liberated and the Nazis defeated. Why did Luther write such things? Should it undermine his position in history? For how long – and to what great extent – had anti-Semitism infected the Church?

As the world emerged from the valley of the shadow of death, the Catholic Church came under scrutiny. We have already seen how Pope Pius XII failed to oppose the rise of Nazism with anything like the vigour of his predecessor, and the common verdict was that his

1948
Israel declares independence

1962 – 1965
Second Vatican Council

1959 – 1975
Vietnam War

1963
Martin Luther King's 'I have a dream'

concerns over communism muted his inner discomfort over the workings of Nazism. Yet after the war Pius did little to reform his image, and attempted to influence the reduction of sentences passed against Nazi war criminals, as well as suggesting that most Germans had been in silent opposition to the Nazis.

Yet it wasn't just Luther and Pius XII who deserved criticism. Anti-semitism had been a default setting in the mind of Christianity for centuries. Many suggest that it was in the twelfth century that Christian anti-Semitism arose, with the blood letting of the first Crusade. Yet anti-Judaism was a prominent feature of many writings during the first millennium: Saint Ambrose, Bishop of Milan, defended the part another bishop played in urging a fourth-century mob to burn a synagogue; Saint Jerome (374-419) railed against the 'Judaic serpents of whom Judas was the model'; Saint Fulgentius of Ruspe in the sixth century lumped the Jewish people in with 'pagans … heretics and schismatics who depart from the present life outside the Catholic Church, are about to go into eternal fire prepared for the devil and his angels.'

Did he mean it? Was he a pre-Nazi? We could get into some technical arguments here, but that would be to miss the point. Christianity had allowed anti-Jewish and anti-Semitic sentiment to grow far too deep for far too long. And after all, for a people whose spiritual beliefs were entwined with every aspect of their identity (unlike those who separated the 'spiritual' from the 'physical' in the Greek manner) to be anti-Judaism was – and is – to be anti-Semitic.

While the Catholic Church would not be far behind, it was the Protestants who first found their voices on this issue. In large part crafted

1966 – 1976
Cultural Revolution, China

1968
Student uprising, France

1969
Apollo 11 Moon landing

1972
Bloody Sunday, Northern Ireland

by Martin Niemoller, The Stuttgart Declaration of Guilt expressed remorse:

> By us infinite wrong was brought over many peoples and countries. That which we often testified to in our communities, we express now in the name of the whole Church: We did fight for long years in the name of Jesus Christ against the mentality that found its awful expression in the National Socialist regime of violence; but we accuse ourselves for not standing to our beliefs more courageously, for not praying more faithfully, for not believing more joyously, and for not loving more ardently.

Niemoller's own biography illustrates the complexity of anti-Semitism within the Church. Despite co-forming the Confessing Church and opposing the endorsement that other German Christians had given Hitler's party – opposition for which he spent the duration of the war in concentration camps – Niemoller had also preached during the 1930s against the Jews: 'What is the reason for [their] obvious punishment, which has lasted for thousands of years? Dear brethren, the reason is easily given: the Jews brought the Christ of God to the cross!'

Even the best of those leading the Church were guilty of complicity, yet what perhaps mattered most was the extent to which Christians accepted responsibility and threw themselves into the rebuilding of society. Since modernism had failed and the earth was once more a little flatter and fairer, the prospect of a new start was not lost on Church leaders.

Prompted by the work of Karl Rahner, the Catholic Church

1948
Israel declares independence

1959 – 1975
Vietnam War

1962 – 1965
Second Vatican Council

1963
Martin Luther King's 'I have a dream'

moved toward its most profound change in too many centuries. Newly elected at the age of 77 in 1959, Pope John XXIII was never supposed to amount to anything more than business as usual. Yet the fact that today he is remembered as 'The Good Pope' should not lead us to imagine that his legacy is bland – anything but. Faced with a world in limbo – one where old modes had failed and new ideals were lining up to assume control – John XXIII called for the Catholic faith to be brought back into the workshop, stripped back, cleaned and put back together again better than it was before.

The Second Vatican Council started in earnest before John XXIII could witness it in full flow; he died in 1963 when discussions were only beginning. Yet the momentum had already been established from the very beginning, when Protestant and Orthodox Eastern Churches were invited to send observers along to the meetings. The four thousand journalists who attended played their part in spreading the message too.

By the time the sessions had concluded in 1965, a wide range of changes had been agreed upon. Finally it was possible for Mass to be conducted around the world in a language other than Latin, bishops were to give considerable more time to engage with pastoral (as opposed to exclusively administrative) issues and laypeople were allowed both bread and wine at the Eucharist. Finally the Jews were absolved of all guilt for the crucifixion and Catholics were urged to devour the bible for themselves, even the Protestant version. Of all the changes, perhaps the most symbolic was the simplest: the priest turned to face the congregation.

Evangelical Churches were experiencing their own period of

1966 – 1976
Cultural Revolution, China

1968
Student uprising, France

1969
Apollo 11 Moon landing

1972
Bloody Sunday, Northern Ireland

renewal as well. As the Holiness movement gathered pace, an increasing number of people experienced dramatic encounters with the Holy Spirit. Whether speaking in tongues or praying for (and experiencing) divine healings, the temperature was increasing – and not just among the usual suspects. Protestant Churches of most denominations were impacted, if only by a few isolated cases. Yet with each minister who experienced a baptism in the power of the Holy Spirit, the charismatic movement spread a little wider.

PROGRESS?

So the revolution was moving forward, yes? Secular society had messed up and the world was about to return to its senses by flooding back to the Church, correct? Not quite. In fact, not at all. The 1960s in Britain saw Church attendance slashed by half, while across the developed world social values left the Church stranded at the altar. Homosexuality and abortion became defining topics for many outside the Church, while for decades those inside either refused to enter the debate or merely stuck to the script of condemnation and unbending thought.

But this is too simplistic a reading of history. The next layer down reveals that there were great advances motivated by Christian values – and by Christians themselves – at this time. One need look no further than the life of Martin Luther King. The single greatest influence in the drive for civil rights during the twentieth century, King's faith was moulded by his Baptist upbringing and his study at the Protestant liberal Crozer Theological Seminary in Pennsylvania, and then at Boston University. Education brought him into contact

1948
Israel declares independence

1962 – 1965
Second Vatican Council

1959 – 1975
Vietnam War

1963
Martin Luther King's 'I have a dream'

with the work of liberal theologian and original instigator of the social gospel, Walter Rauschenbusch. King declared that he 'had done a great service for the Christian Church by insisting that the gospel deals with the whole man, not only his soul but his body'.

Later, this approach would evolve into the Integral Mission movement of the early 2020s, but for now – in the middle of the cultural maelstrom of the 1960s – King's application of the gospel to the needs of the whole individual had a radical impact. Energising crowds through a series of inspired speeches and practical methods of non-violent resistance, he first tackled the system of segregation that kept black and white apart physically. Later, King moved on to oppose the wholly unpopular Vietnam War, as well as to address the crises in housing, employment, health and education that trapped so many in his country.

For the man who co-pastored his father's Ebenezer Baptist Church in Atlanta, charges of marital infidelity did little to dent his impact, even though the charges were fair and true. While some struggled to accept him as a true Church leader, his assassination in 1968 prompted a national day of mourning.

At King's funeral, his wife chose to play a recording of his last sermon delivered at Ebenezer Baptist Church. In it, King asked that at his funeral there be no focus on his achievements or awards, but that it be said that his life was given over to attempts to 'feed the hungry', 'clothe the naked', 'be right on the war question', and 'love and serve humanity'.

Elsewhere, the Church was having an impact upon society in dramatic ways, particularly in South America. Liberation theology

1966 – 1976
Cultural Revolution, China

1968
Student uprising, France

1969
Apollo 11 Moon landing

1972
Bloody Sunday, Northern Ireland

unpicked the assumption that the Church needed first to pursue its theology along intellectual lines before putting it into action. Instead, went the argument, social injustices should be tackled first, with the talking about it only following after.

At the front of the queue, bringing social change and deferring the theological ruminations was Father Camilo Torres Restrepo, a man who held the unique place in history of being both a Roman Catholic priest and a member of the National Liberation Army (ELN) guerrilla group. Killed during his first military engagement (ambushing a Colombian military patrol), his life's work was devoted to the bridging of the gap between Marxism and Christianity, and his legacy extends beyond the soundbite most people remember him by: 'If Jesus were alive today, He would be a *guerrillero*.'

Tores was not the first to see the links between Christianity and communism. Many who looked back to the era of nineteenth-century social activism wondered whether communism in some form might offer a quick link back to the days of the early Church as described in the book of Acts. However, while plenty wondered, those with power made sure that religion held next to no power at all in communist states. Blame Karl Marx if you like – the arch-atheist had no time at all for belief in God – although the guilt for the persecution of Christians living in communist regimes must be shared among a wider pool.

Joseph Stalin was nothing if not efficient. Under his watch the Russian Orthodox Church was decimated. Theological schools were closed, Church publications prohibited and nearly all of its clergy, and many of its believers, were shot or sent to labour camps. Between 1917

1948
Israel declares independence

1959 – 1975
Vietnam War

1962 – 1965
Second Vatican Council

1963
Martin Luther King's 'I have a dream'

and 1935, 130,000 Orthodox priests were arrested, and of these, 95,000 were executed by firing squad. The Russian Orthodox Church survived only by retreating underground and keeping very, very quiet.

As the postwar period demanded retreat and basic rehabilitation, between 1945 and 1959 the official organisation of the Church was greatly expanded. Of course, individual members of the clergy were occasionally arrested and exiled, but it remained a comparatively open time for Christians living beneath Mother Russia's austere arms. The number of open churches increased to 25,000, but the growth was short lived. In 1959 Nikita Khrushchev started his own campaign against the Russian Orthodox Church, forcing half of them to close and executing an estimated 50,000 clergy. But Krushchev knew the value of the institution, and so replaced those he had killed with his own 'docile' clergy, many of whom had ties with the shadowy security force known as the KGB.

Religious persecution was not limited to those in Russia. The Ukrainian Greek Catholic Church found itself absorbed by the Soviet Bloc, and was duly terrorised in 1945, while Albania was declared the first atheist state in the world in 1967, and believers in Czechoslovakia found every aspect of their faith taken over entirely by the state.

Elsewhere in the world, experiments in communism followed a similar path, with some 300 Catholic clergy killed in Mexico and 8,000 murdered by communist soldiers in Spain. In 1949 it was the turn of China to turn to communism, taking theirs with the usual double shot of atheism. Between 1949 and 1952, all foreign missionaries left the country, reluctantly, but with a clear knowledge of what

1966 – 1976
Cultural Revolution, China

1968
Student uprising, France

1969
Apollo 11 Moon landing

1972
Bloody Sunday, Northern Ireland

would happen if they stayed. During the Cultural Revolution of 1966 to 1976, religious life in China was effectively banned. Believers were arrested and imprisoned, sometimes tortured and even killed. Bibles were destroyed; churches and homes looted, and Christians were subjected to humiliation and abuse.

Perhaps this slightly less brutal approach from the authorities allowed the Church in China to do more than just survive, as it did in Russia. Amid the uniforms and the little red books and the official policies there emerged the Chinese house church movement. There were striking parallels with the early, pre-Constantine Church: believers feared persecution and met in their homes, the only real places that they could be sure offered safety. When, in 1979, the government officially restored the one formal Church that it had earlier authorised – the Protestant Three Self Patriotic Movement – it did not take long for the Church's influence to be made clear. By 1993 there were seven million members of the TSPM with eleven million affiliated. But that was nothing compared to those aligned to unauthorised Protestant Churches; an estimated eighteen million and forty-seven million respectively.

So being a Christian in China during the twentieth century was one of two extremes: exceedingly good or exceptionally bad. Reacting to decades of colonial rule by distant western nations, the extreme nationalist group known as The Boxers gathered momentum. Uniting under the slogan 'Support the Qing and destroy the foreigners' they launched an unsuccessful rebellion. Yet while they failed to gain power, they left an audacious body count in their wake, including 188 foreign missionaries and 32,000 Chinese Christians slaughtered for their faith.

These events were horrific. But from the 32,188 stories comes a

1948
Israel declares independence

1959 – 1975
Vietnam War

1962 – 1965
Second Vatican Council

1963
Martin Luther King's 'I have a dream'

seemingly endless supply of tales of courage, compassion and premium-grade faith. Like the tale of the Chinese pastor who refused to recant his faith. Incensed by his stand, the mob cut off his eyebrows, lips and ears. When he still refused to deny his faith, they wrenched his heart from his body. The pastor's fourteen-year-old daughter saw it all yet refused turn her back on Christ, sharing her father's fate as well as his faith.

The Boxers were intent on ridding their land of the 'white devils', and were convinced they had caught and could humiliate another one as they tied a pastor to a pillar inside a pagan temple. All night the man preached to his captors. Morning brought with it an angry mob, one-thousand strong. Again they tore out his heart.

The same crowd in Tsun-hua chopped the feet off an 'uncooperative' Chinese Christian teacher, while a colleague implored her pupils to 'keep the faith' as she was burned alive.

There's something about the sacrifice of martyrs that inspires, forcing those who trade in their stories like currency to ask how far they would go for their own beliefs. The nineteenth-century Polish poet Cyprian Norwid understood this. According to him a truly fulfilling life must contain three essential requirements: 'something to live on, something to live for, and something to die for'. He went on: 'The lack of one of these attributes results in drama. The lack of two results in tragedy.'

***

While the Chinese Christians found that persecution at home slowly began to ease off, and their support from overseas increased, other

1966 – 1976
Cultural Revolution, China

1968
Student uprising, France

1969
Apollo 11 Moon landing

1972
Bloody Sunday, Northern Ireland

Christians were dying for far less noble reasons. Ireland was split into a nominally Protestant north and Catholic south in 1922, yet the real story was more complex. Politics, a history of oppression and a taste for lethal violence combined to produce the Troubles. For three decades violence raged as Catholic republicans battled Protestant loyalists, with British army soldiers swaying between the dual roles of enforcers of the peace and perpetrators of the crimes. In all some 3,500 people lost their lives at the hands of bombers, shooters, lynchers and raging mobs. It was a brutal period that devastated the region – in particular the city of Belfast – and one which the Church seemed utterly powerless to put right. Eventually the slow shuffle towards political peace was begun in the 1990s, but it was not for another forty years that Christianity would be able to offer anything like the leadership the divided country needed.

Elsewhere the fighting in the name of religion continued, refusing to ease as generations were born into – and taken out of – a life scarred by violence. In the years after the Second World War – after almost a century of increasing Jewish settlement back in the area known as the Holy Land – the United Nations tried and failed to create two states (one Arab, on Jewish) out of the area known as Palestine. Israel declared itself a state anyway in 1948, and its opponents lined up to fight. From then on the battles continued throughout the rest of the century and beyond. At times Israel gained a little more land, at other times the Muslim attackers appeared to be gaining the upper hand. Yet as long as the west continued to support Israel – motivated in large part by the enormous sense of collective guilt felt about the Holocaust – it managed to maintain its independence in the region.

Chapter Twelve

1984 – 2001
A Cold Dawn

It appeared to happen almost overnight; the iron curtain fell and communism effectively left the building. The greatest experiment in state-directed atheism failed to fulfil its central objective; to provide for the needs of those within its borders. Shops were empty, hope was gone and freedom was just another rumour that filtered through from the decadent west.

Depending on your politics, the fall of communism began with the reforms of President Mikhail Gorbachev or with the very first leaders such as Lenin and Stalin. For the sake of argument, it is easier to see Gorbachev's hand in the decline, particularly in his policies of *glasnost* (openness) and *perestroika* (restructuring). Having experienced the harsh realities of life for the ordinary Russian labourer – as well as the brutalities of Stalin's rule when his grandfather was sentenced to nine years in the gulag labour camps for not giving enough grain to the collective harvest – Gorbachev was clearly minded to bring change to Russia. By encouraging private ownership of businesses, ending the one-party system and promoting free speech, his signals were clear. When, in 1988 he ended the Brezhnev Doctrine – a policy that bound Russia in to interfere in the affairs of eastern bloc countries should they begin to wander too far from communist ideals – the Cold War died with it.

Within months the Poles had voted out the communists, the East German government collapsed – along with it the in famous Berlin Wall that had divided city and family alike – and Nicolae Ceausescu (a dictator who had learnt much from Stalin) was overthrown and executed by the Czechoslovakian people.

1986
Chernobyl nuclear disaster, USSR

1986
Live Aid concert

1989
Tian'anmen Square massacre, China

1989
Berlin Wall torn down

The Church had been active throughout the build up to these events. The Russian Orthodox Church had remained a prime example of quiet defiance in the face of grotesque abuse, while Poland's long and wealthy heritage as a Catholic nation was brought to a bright new dawn with the election of Karol Wojtyla as Pope John Paul II. Wojtyla had experienced Nazi rule and communist oppression, and brought to the Vatican an awareness of the Church's role within the drive for social change. Thanks to people like him – as well as the countless anonymous believers who allowed their faith to shape their actions in spite of great personal risk – the ripples of transformation spread across the world, and the west's fear of nuclear annihilation at the hands of cold-blooded Russian killers suddenly seemed quaint and out of touch.

So the world was changing for the better. In China, India and Africa Christianity hurtled towards the end of the second millennium with ever-increasing optimism and sense of self. Many Christians in South Africa had largely been indifferent to the injustice of apartheid. Others had not; they had been involved from the start. The Dutch Reformed Church helped plan, implement and legitimise apartheid, with Reverend J. G. Strijdom claiming in 1938 that '… there are people who falsely maintain on biblical grounds that apartheid is wrong. We, however, believe on the basis of God's word that he has willed nations to be apart.'

However, by 1986 the tides were shifting, and the South African Dutch Reformed Church had its membership suspended by the

1990 – 1991
Gulf War

1994
Rwandan genocide

1994
Toronto Blessing, Canada

1997
Mother Teresa dies

World Alliance of Reformed Churches. Theology had made its way out from the whites-only gated communities and into the squalor of the townships. There, envisioned by the likes of Steve Biko, emancipation was seen as both mental and physical, with whites and blacks alike in need of a clearer vision of God's harmony. Biko was killed in police custody in 1977 and declared a Christian martyr soon after. Within less than two decades apartheid was over and Nelson Mandela sworn in as the country's first black president.

South and Central America followed similar paths, with social injustice challenged by the continuing developments within liberation theology. On the front lines was Oscar Romero, Archbishop of San Salvador in El Salvador and a vocal opponent of the human rights abuses carried out against both the poor and the Church during the country's civil war. He paid with his life in 1980, assassinated while conducting mass, and at his funeral a week later mourners dodged bullets and bombs. The army was accused and considered guilty by most.

While revolution had not been required in Italy, the arrival of the new pope in 1978 was dramatic news. John Paul I was rumoured to be too progressive for the conservative power brokers, and his positions on contraception and support for poorer countries made him unpopular. Still, if this was surprising, it was nothing compared to what happened after 33 days of his papacy. He died. Found sitting up in bed one morning, it was assumed that the sixty-five-year-old had suffered a heart attack in the night, yet with no autopsy performed the rumours abounded. And so John Paul I's

1986
Chernobyl nuclear disaster, USSR

1986
Live Aid concert

1989
Tian'anmen Square massacre, China

1989
Berlin Wall torn down

name was added to the list of Popes allegedly murdered. He was the tenth. Incidentally, the list of those known to have been murdered is a little shorter; just eight, with the most recent being Pope Pius XXIII in 2103.

ISMS

The Church was changing. Throughout the twentieth century many had been working to reunite and restore relationships between denominations fractured across the centuries. The ecumenical movement made good progress, starting with the 1920 World Mission Conference and ending the century with a series of successes; American Anglicans and Lutherans, Methodists and Anglicans, Lutherans and Roman Catholics all moved closer together by resolving differences on a range of issues. The Pentecostals and Charismatic Evangelicals largely stayed away from the party, their growing numbers reducing the sense of urgency that drove others towards ecumenicalism.

While many drove to the centre in search of common ground, the gap between liberal and conservative theology was growing ever wider. While liberalism started with the rejection of traditional doctrines, the opposition had a clear path ahead; re-emphasise the importance of such fundamental doctrines. In doing so these conservative Protestants boiled Christianity down to what they saw as the essential truths without which nobody could truly claim faith: that the bible was incontrovertibly right, that God's son Jesus was born of a virgin, died, rose again and would come back to rule the earth. Fundamentalism was born.

1990 – 1991
Gulf War

1994
Rwandan genocide

1994
Toronto Blessing, Canada

1997
Mother Teresa dies

Not all evangelicals closed their ears and minds to the questions of the liberal theologians, but the ones who did had by far the loudest voices. Christian fundamentalism became synonymous with the political right and the simple dualistic doctrine was ripe for TV broadcast. A new breed of Christian preacher emerged – the televangelist. With their syndicated sermons, talk of the end of the world and promises of healing and prosperity for those who exhibited the correct degree of faith (often evidenced by sending in a donation to said televangelist), their popularity soared, but only among a certain demographic. The fundamentalist message was nectar to the poor and uneducated, those who felt left out on the fringes of society. Jerry Falwell, Jimmy Swaggart and a host of other white-toothed, expensively-suited 'ministers' fed the people exactly what they wanted to hear. And when the AIDS virus was discovered among the gay community in 1981, it was as if Christmas had come early. Here, at last was a clear indication of God's judgement upon the very kind of people that the televangelists had been railing against for years.

But if the televangelists grew rich – and they did; obscenely so – it was not a reflection of truly widespread popularity. Rather, it pointed to their abilities to prise exorbitant amounts of money from people who could ill afford it. While their – largely American – audience reached out and touched the screen, those living outside of the fundamentalist Christian bubble looked on aghast. The transition from modernism to postmodernism had created an environment where large institutions were viewed with mistrust. Yet while

1986
Chernobyl nuclear disaster, USSR

1986
Live Aid concert

1989
Tian'anmen Square massacre, China

1989
Berlin Wall torn down

conspiracy theories were crafted to expose cracks in governments, no such paranoia was needed when it came to the Church; there, in glorious Technicolor, was all the evidence that many would ever need to discount the Church as irrelevant, self-obsessed and distinctly unpleasant.

Of course not all evangelicals were fundamentalists, and not all fundamentalists went as far along the them/us mode of thinking personified by the white men in suits on the TV screen. But as the century ended the Church's decline appeared to be entering a terminal phase. Christianity had shifted from being something that raged against injustice to a curio of little significance and even less relevance. What possible need could a person have for such introspective and outdated ideals? With their values shaped by an increasingly sophisticated advertising industry, many in the west simply moved on.

FAILINGS

As well as the wealth and the hypocrisy, the bile and the bigotry, Christianity was guilty of a range of crimes. Mirroring the materialistic culture celebrated within the new cathedrals of shopping malls, the Church became a highly profitable business. The facts of Christian publishing were nothing new, and long before John Wesley made thousands from book sales there had been Christians who had made money from other Christians. But this was something new; from prayer shawls to bible covers, ancient Hebrew trumpets to t-shirts, the rise of Christian retailing saw business-minded individuals stop at nothing to make a profit. And

1990 – 1991
Gulf War

1994
Toronto Blessing, Canada

1994
Rwandan genocide

1997
Mother Teresa dies

because it was all under the banner of 'equipping the Church', even the most banal items were loaded with heavenly significance. Why would any Christian even consider leaving the house without the bracelet around their wrist asking them *wwjd?* – 'What would Jesus do?'.

It wasn't all eye-rollingly-embarrassing; some of it was utterly wrong and awful, like the Roman Catholic sex abuse scandals. Having spent decades covering up the abuse of minors – as well as adults – by priests, teachers and leaders, something broke with the eruption of the scandal in Boston, USA in 2002. The perpetrators were high up, even the then-Cardinal Bernard Law was found guilty of moving priests on to new parishes rather than defrocking or reporting them to the authorities. Similar reports surfaced across the globe, with as many as 11,000 people having accused priests in the US of child sexual abuse in the second half of the twentieth century. The Boston Diocese, facing over one thousand court cases, shut more than sixty churches in Massachusetts in order to help raise the $85 million compensation bill. One by one many dioceses filed for bankruptcy, while on the west coast, the Archdiocese of Los Angeles agreed to pay $660 million to 500 victims of sexual abuse dating as far back as the 1940s, the largest compensation deal of its kind.

In Austria, Australia, Ireland and beyond, the stories continued to emerge, every one unique for those abused but bearing the same old DNA: the abuse by those in power and the attempts to cover up or ignore it by those above them. The double betrayal cost the Church dear.

1986
Chernobyl nuclear disaster, USSR

1986
Live Aid concert

1989
Tian'anmen Square massacre, China

1989
Berlin Wall torn down

Many of those who emerged as leading televangelists found themselves caught up in scandal and publicly humiliated. While scandal and humiliation were not exactly strangers to the Church, the rise and fall of these fundamentalists made for excellent newspaper copy.

Time and time again the once-righteous preachers fell in utterly human ways. In 1986, evangelist Jimmy Swaggart used his TV slots to attack fellow televangelists Marvin Gorman and Jim Bakker. He uncovered Gorman's affair with a Church member, and helped expose Bakker's infidelity. Gorman hit back by hiring a private investigator to uncover Swaggart's own liaisons with a prostitute. Swaggart confessed, cried and stepped down, only to get caught out again with another prostitute in California three years later.

For Peter Popoff, however, it wasn't his libido that lured him into trouble. In an attempt to appear a credible prophet and faith healer, Popoff suggested that it was direct from God that he received personal information about the individuals in the audience he would single out and pray for. The truth was slightly less inspiring; it was his wife, via an in-ear-receiver, who was providing the necessary reading out of the prayer cards filled out by the faithful prior to the service. Once exposed, his $4million annual income vanished overnight.

Despite the handful of scandals, their impact was significant. Yet the charlatans were not alone in their guilt. As the west grew richer so too did the gulf of injustice between the rich and those living in what was then known as the Third World. AIDS spread

1990 – 1991
Gulf War

1994
Toronto Blessing, Canada

1994
Rwandan genocide

1997
Mother Teresa dies

across the globe, claiming millions of lives each year, and not just among gay men as Falwell and others had assumed earlier on. Millions of children were orphaned by HIV, infected themselves, or simply forced into a cycle of death as poverty and disease throttled entire nations. Extreme poverty brought with it extreme hunger, and while the west consumed resources without seeming to spare a thought for the planet, individuals living in regions like sub-Saharan Africa were left to die. And all along, the Church had nothing to say.

There can hardly be a better example than the genocide that took place in Rwanda in 1994. Long considered to be one of the most 'Christian' countries in Africa, some 80% to 90% of the population regarded themselves as Christians, most of them Roman Catholic, but many evangelical Protestant. When the underdog Hutu rose to bring down the ruling Tutsi, the Catholic Church failed to condemn the violence. Some clergy offered protection, but many more turned a blind eye or even helped the killers to turn churches from places of refuge into open abattoirs.

The rest of the world did little better. Governments parsed their words and avoided calling it genocide, for fear of having to intervene for real. Yet as the body count topped 800,000 in just 100 days, the horror gradually dawned on world leaders and the French stepped in to quell the killing.

From 1991 to 2001 war also shattered the Balkans. As in Rwanda the fighting was along ethnic lines, yet in this case religion played an active part. Serbian Orthodox Christians pursued a policy of ethnic 'cleansing', driving European Muslims away, using rape as a frequent

1986
Chernobyl nuclear disaster, USSR

1986
Live Aid concert

1989
Tian'anmen Square massacre, China

1989
Berlin Wall torn down

weapon of choice. All along, the Church was either silent or powerless; neither of which seem like an appropriate mode of conduct.

DISTRACTION

Many evangelicals discovered throughout the 1980s and 1990s that the world within the Church walls was a far safer place to be than out beyond the car park. The world of gay rights, abortion, drugs, immigration and loosening social values was both alien and frightening for many. The Church, on the other had, provided more than an alternative code by which to live, but a real sense that if the world was to be put right, putting the hours in at church was an absolute essential. Following on from the revivals that peppered Scotland, Wales and Los Angeles in the eighteenth and early-nineteenth centuries, the western evangelical Church entered a period of increased activity that many pointed to as evidence of revival, starting in the 1960s and increasing in pace with the passing decades. The Church of England was particularly impacted in the 1980s through the work of the Californian Vineyard founder, John Wimber, as well as David Watson and Michael Harper (who later left the Church of England and moved to the Greek Orthodox Church). From that point there followed interest and derision in equal measure, and across the globe the renewal movement gathered pace. Leaving out the prosperity teaching that had been absorbed by many Pentecostal Churches, the Charismatic movement embraced the signs of emotional connection. Speaking in tongues, divine healing and prophecy were all experienced

1990 – 1991
Gulf War

1994
Toronto Blessing, Canada

1994
Rwandan genocide

1997
Mother Teresa dies

beneath an overarching assumption that since God was real, his Holy Spirit had plenty to say to his people. At various times the intensity increased, with one season that started at a church in Toronto being marked by strange behaviour accredited widely as being a response to the presence of God. So people laughed, barked, clucked and bobbed around church halls for hours on end, desperate to 'catch the fire' again and again.

It was something of a party, but one held behind closed doors. Poverty continued to claim lives needlessly, culture continued to shift further away and still the Christians laughed, barked, clucked and bobbed. Scolded by a woman who had left the comfort of wealthy London for the squalor of a life among drug addicts within Hong Kong's Walled City, the Church listened as Jackie Pullinger delivered her verdict of the so-called Toronto Blessing: 'When we heard that people were jumping on planes to go to the place where the laughing was we thought that it would not be long before they boarded planes to come to the places where the crying is. We waited. You never came.'

Not all revivals were myopic. In a remote part of northern Australia, an Aboriginal community had experienced repeatedly intense reactions within it meetings. At various times in its history the church at Yarrabah had been a remarkable force for social change among the community. For a year the local bar had to close down due to lack of trade, and the instances of drug abuse and domestic violence flew in the face of national trends. At other points the church was just another church; half filled with Christians in search of community and connection. It never

1986
Chernobyl nuclear disaster, USSR

1986
Live Aid concert

1989
Tian'anmen Square massacre, China

1989
Berlin Wall torn down

made the headlines at the time, but Yarrabah's revival proved to be a compass by which future churches would evaluate their experience of moves of the Holy Spirit. The Yarrabah Questions would become famous: Who is it for? What will it change? How can we serve? Decades later, the crowds would flock there in search of answers.

SMALL STEPS

She was twelve when it happened. Still a child, yet something within her had shifted; the first seeds of a dream had taken root. Her family was wealthy – with two homes and a father who was a successful building contractor – but grief had left its scars. Of the five children born to the girl's parents only three had survived. And when she was seven, Gonxha Bojaxhiu's father had died suddenly – suspiciously, some said, hinting that his political activism may have earned him dangerous enemies. But it was when she was just twelve that the change happened. It was then, only five years on from his death, that Gonxha – known as Agnes – became fascinated by a simple idea that her life should be spent serving others. That was all it took to transform her life and set her on course for a remarkable life of simple acts.

If there's such a thing as a missionary geek, Agnes was it. Give her a map and even as a teenager she'd put on a good show, pointing out locations of missions and the work they carried out. Of course, these plans took time to evolve, and it took another five years for the reality to kick in. It was then when she was 18 that she left her home and travelled the 1500 miles from Yugoslavia to Dublin, Ireland. Agnes

1990 – 1991
Gulf War

1994
Rwandan genocide

1994
Toronto Blessing, Canada

1997
Mother Teresa dies

had taken yet another small step which would lead her closer to pain, compassion, Christ and the poor.

It turned out that 1928 was an eventful year. The world was shaken by assassinations in Mexico and Yugoslavia, an earthquake destroyed Corinth, Fleming discovered penicillin, Opus Dei was founded and Lindberg and Earhart found glory in the skies. But in the midst of it all Agnes was with the Loreto Sisters in Ireland, preparing for her departure to Darjeeling, India, and a life she assumed would be shaped by her work as a teacher of the daughters of the wealthy.

The thing about Agnes is that she eventually became a household name. She had to change that name, but generations that followed all knew how Saint Teresa's story developed. Her work among the poor of Calcutta, India; the Nobel peace prize; the global celebrity and the quiet, whispered death that was overshadowed by the tragedy of an English princess killed as her car crashed while being chased by photographers in Paris. Saint Teresa became known as the symbol of Christian goodness and charity, of humility and sacrifice, as a legend who became a saint in 2026, as a symbol of how much the human spirit can achieve.

A few cynics aside, the world paused for a second and mourned the death of Saint Teresa by declaring her life a true success. She died poor, but her legacy was shared among millions. In a world where the Church was in danger of getting lost among its own halls of power, Saint Teresa illuminated a better path for people to take.

A cynical journalist once asked her why she did what she did.

'What's the point of all this?' asked the sceptic. 'Aren't all your

1986
Chernobyl nuclear disaster, USSR

1989
Tian`anmen Square massacre, China

1986
Live Aid concert

1989
Berlin Wall torn down

good works merely a drop in the ocean?'

'Ah yes,' came the reply. 'But the ocean is made up of many drops.'

The exchange – probably apocryphal – reveals much about the culture of the day. The journalist took offence at Saint Teresa's assumption that she could – and ought to – do something about the injustices that surrounded her. It was a common enough complaint – that the problems of other people are other people's problems – but his words go deeper and get more personal than that. The hack was complaining not only about the work of the Sisters of Charity among the poor, but the fact that Saint Teresa and those like her would overcome the apathy *within* and start to live in an opposite spirit to that which was visible around them. This was a controversial message for a society that outsourced everything from cooking to childcare. Contemporary culture was conditioned to prefer the end result to the process, to favour whatever was instant or immediately impressive over that which was hard won and hidden from public view. To measure our lives in small steps or drops in oceans went against much of the culture of the day.

Years later, when fame had done nothing to alter her outlook and global recognition failed to turn her head, Saint Teresa tried to resign from her position as head of the Sisters of Charity. She was too old, she said, too frail. It was time for someone else to take over. So the order held a secret ballot. Only one vote was cast in support of her stepping down. It was her own.

Small steps were all it took. For Saint Teresa her path was marked by constant decisions to take the time and expend the energy in

1990 – 1991
Gulf War

1994
Toronto Blessing, Canada

1994
Rwandan genocide

1997
Mother Teresa dies

caring for those that society would have preferred her to forget. It would take years for them to reach their full potential, but these small steps were to scale some sizeable mountains.

Chapter Thirteen

2001 – 2019
The Storm Before the Calm

The days of secularisation began to fade with the dawning of the third millennium. What many at the time considered to be a safe bet for the future of civilisation – a world where religion would be nothing more than a cultural oddity, forever robbed of its mass power and appeal – turned out to be a wholly false prediction. Instead of becoming less religious, much of mainstream western culture found itself on a pilgrimage back towards faith.

Not that secularism went down without a fight. The early years of the twenty-first century saw a growth in popular atheism. Like the darkest days of the Dark Ages it appeared at times as though there were too few voices prepared to defend the value of faith. Belief that God either failed to exist or was too weak to summon up the power to be of any use to anyone became increasingly dominant. Everything from film to pulp fiction, weekend editions of printed newspapers to lists of bestselling hardback books picked up the scent. As commentators reached back to the likes of Mark Twain, Karl Marx and Freud, it was as if a century of doubt lined up the final nails to be inserted into the coffin. Surely this was the end of religion once and for all?

Yet there is a paradox surrounding the growth of atheism: increasing popularity brought with it decreasing potency. In 1882 it was only the emboldened renegades such as Friedrich Nietzsche who articulated the sentiment with the words 'God is dead!'. In the late 1960s the cry was reserved for characters in horror films based on satanic ritual, such as *Rosemary's Baby* – a novel in 1967 and a film in 1968. Forty years later these three words barely raised an eyebrow.

Leading the charge were the likes of Richard Dawkins and Christopher Hitchens. Both authors scored big sales with books such

2001
Terrorist attacks on USA

2008 – 2011
Depression 2.0

2013
Increased terrorist activity begins

2014
Anglican Communion split

as *The God Delusion* (Dawkins, 2006) and *God Is Not Great* (Hitchens, 2007), yet it is Dawkins whom history chooses to remember with the greater clarity. Not, however, for his acerbic atheism, but for his dramatic conversion in later life to an obscure branch of Orthodox Christianity, the Jacobite Syrian Christian Church. While still an opponent of evangelicalism, Dawkins' final work – *The Learning Gene* (2021) – charted his religious conversion, albeit with slightly less bluster and arrogance than his earlier works.

As has already been explored, the rise of secularism towards the end of the second millennium had roots that trailed back over the previous two centuries. From the Age of Enlightenment onwards, religion was under attack, brought on largely by many of its own failings and misjudgements. Yet as the twenty-first century took its first steps there were unique influences at work. While for two hundred years religion and politics had been drifting apart, events in the United States of America on Tuesday September 11th, 2001 dramatically altered history's course. The infamous terrorist attacks claimed 2,974 lives, and in the immediate aftermath a relatively short-lived and largely unsuccessful war on terror was waged. Over the coming years the rhetoric took on an increasingly religious tone, with President George W. Bush leading his country in a crusade against the 'axis of evil'. At home that meant registering and finger-printing 80,000 Muslim and Arab immigrants, while actions overseas took a far graver course. The military interventions in Afghanistan, Iraq and Iran became visible symbols of the increasing battle between political and religious ideals.

For many the so-called 'war on terror' serves as proof of the

2016
H5N1 mutates into HN73

2017
High point of Christian activism on poverty

2017 – 2018
Sub-Saharan Africa devastated by drought

2017 – 2018
Fossil fuel estimates revised significantly downwards

complete failure of religion – the embarrassing final fight from two heavyweights who should have long ago realised their frailty. As Christianity took on Islam, the body count rose and political stability decreased. A pox on both their houses, cried the commentators, both camps are religious fanatics and the sooner we are rid of them the better.

Yet tempting as it is to read it this way an alternative reaction was gathering pace: the role of religious dogma in acts of terrorism, as well as the co-opting of a right-wing political agenda, left others with an impression that faith was capable of a far greater degree of integrity. In other words, it served to stiffen the resolve of the faithful to ensure that religion revolved around higher standards. The results of this took years to filter through, but the groundswell began in part with the opposition to the politics and terrorism of the early twenty-first century. The 'Not In My Name' movement, which started as a set of homemade placards at anti-war rallies in 2002, eventually became the rallying cry of Muslims and Christians the world over – their words directed out to those on the fringe who had hijacked their faith.

THE RIGHT GONE WRONG

Some within the Church seemed to be doing their best to drive Christianity towards the cliff-face. The USA had been home to the rise of the Religious Right; conservative Christians from a variety of denominations, but with an increasing tendency towards evangelicalism. Active since the 1960s, but with particularly high visibility since Jerry Falwell's creation of the Moral Majority in 1979, they

2001
Terrorist attacks on USA

2008 – 2011
Depression 2.0

2013
Increased terrorist activity begins

2014
Anglican Communion split

were highly politically active, especially when it came to defending their core values of being opposed to abortion, gay marriage and the teaching of evolution in schools. An aggressive foreign policy (with particular support for the State of Israel, which they saw as pivotal to the imminent return of Christ) and reductions in the state's role as provider of social welfare also helped give them clear lines of definition.

In Australia, Canada, New Zealand and the United Kingdom, the religious right gained notoriety and influence. They pushed hard for clocks to be turned back, fought wars in the name of what was right and appeared every inch the authoritarian leaders who would never release their grip on power. Yet change often comes quickly, and in the case of the Religious Right the world shifted before many had even realised.

To the casual observer that change occurred with the election of Senator Barack Obama as 44th President of the United States of America. The election was a straight up or down choice over the future of the country; bi-racial, protestant Obama represented change while his white, 72-year-old rival (accompanied by what was considered by a dwindling minority to be the archetypal Religious Right pinup girl as Vice Presidential nominee) offered little more than a re-run of what had gone before. The country chose change, but Obama was a symptom of the shift in values rather than the cause. While previous Republican administrations had learnt to court and count on the support of the Religious Right, by 2008 the exodus was well and truly underway.

The dawn of the new millennium (although technically a year

2016
H5N1 mutates into HN73

2017 – 2018
Sub-Saharan Africa devastated by drought

2017
High point of Christian activism on poverty

2017 – 2018
Fossil fuel estimates revised significantly downwards

early) proved to be a key milestone in the life of the Church. The Jubilee Debt campaign did something remarkable within the life of many Christians, ripping down old assumptions that politics was best left to the politicians and that faith was best preserved within the Church. Christians in their thousands were marching, campaigning and badgering politicians once more, and the biggest change of all was the subject of their protest. Instead of declining moral standards or an erosion of Christianity's status, they were active on behalf of the world's silent majority, trapped by poverty and overlooked by the wealthy.

Christian social activism had never vanished completely since its highpoint in the nineteenth century, but many in the evangelical Church had never before grasped the message so clearly – at least, not in their lifetime had the Church been so engaged with tackling social problems. In the years that followed it became increasingly common for Churches to teach on, and respond to, subjects as diverse as climate change, poverty, AIDS, water and sanitation and the horrors of sex trafficking. Within a couple of decades such messages moved from being peripheral concerns associated with social and theological liberals to being the bedrock of many mainstream protestant and catholic's involvement within society.

The days of scandalous apathy and greed were gradually fading. While some continued to dupe their flock into parting with significant amounts of money, others – like Texan Pastor John Hagee – took the bold step of urging pre-emptive strikes upon middle eastern states in defence of Israel. Yet Hagee and his like were a dying breed. Scandal took care of a few – like the infamous financial scams of Benny Hinn – while the United States Senate conducted a series of investigations, starting in 2007, into the financial dealings of those who claimed tax exempt status. Others simply faded further from the public eye, preaching prosperity like ageing boxers, a little undignified and dangerous to none but themselves, unable to do anything else.

SPLIT

In 2001 a mere third of the world's population were Christians. While those two billion believers represented the largest of the major world religions, few at the time felt as though they were part of a united movement. In spite of such low numbers the Christian faith in the earl- twentieth century was about to experience significant change. Call it pre-transition, warm-up or shake-down, the title is irrelevant, what matters is that from 2002 onwards the Church was caught up in a dramatic shift. Though the agnostic observer may have believed that the mainstream's attacks on the existence of God left the Church cowering in a corner, the bulk of the world's believers had other issues to discuss.

From 2001 to 2019 the Church was dominated by key struggles, formative shifts in the plates of faith that left the landscape forever changed. At the top of the list were two issues which dictated the future course of the faith; the way that the Church responded to those who were gay and the way that it responded to those who were poor. While the reaction to one of these topics served to fuel a significant renewal of the Church's influence and growth, the failure to deal effectively with the other dealt the global Church a blow from which it took the best part of a century to recover.

2016
H5N1 mutates into HN73

2017 – 2018
Sub-Saharan Africa devastated by drought

2017
High point of Christian activism on poverty

2017 – 2018
Fossil fuel estimates revised significantly downwards

The tale of the global Church's struggle to find a united response to its approach to homosexuality can be told in a large part through one man's experiences. Elected in 2002, the struggles began almost immediately for the 104th Archbishop of Canterbury, Dr Rowan Williams. What had been a largely private debate ignited into a full-scale war, a series of battles, skirmishes and eventually even the odd suicide mission.

It started in 2003 when the Anglican body in the United States of America – a carcass formerly known as the Episcopal Church – appointed the openly gay Gene Robinson Bishop of New Hampshire. This did not go down well. In fact, it went down spectacularly badly among some of the other 79 million members of the worldwide Anglican Communion. Chief among them was Nigerian Archbishop Peter Akinola. His view that God regards homosexuality on a par with bestiality gained him much support, particularly among fellow African and Asian Anglicans. His stance towards Williams also did him no harm, with Akinola publicly declaring that 'We don't have to go through Canterbury to get to Jesus.' In setting up his own Anglican body in the USA — the Convocation of Anglicans in North America (CANA) — the Nigerian Archbishop thumbed his nose at Williams. Yet the Welshman's soft baritone reply remained constant: the Church should find and focus on that which unites it rather than that which divides.

In searching for a figure to blame for the tensions within the Church, one could do worse than to point the finger at the rapid advances in communication technology of the time. The fresh appetite for instant news, user-generated content and free-flowing opinions created a previously unfamiliar tension for many around the world. Suddenly conservative communities could see what their liberal cousins had been up to the day before and liberals finally got to hear what their conservative comrades thought of the way they behaved. The global Anglican Communion quickly discovered once more that, like many families, the presence of diversity and difference under one roof is a difficult situation to resolve.

As soon as the Gene Robinson consecration took place observers lined up to predict the precise point at which the Church would split. For the best part of a decade Williams managed to hold the clouds together, but at times it appeared as if it was only by sheer force of hope, will and desperation. The fight, of course, eventually became too much for just one man. Williams' subsequent ill-health plagued his second decade in office, dominated by the formal split within the Anglican Communion in 2014. Almost overnight as many as thirty-three million members found themselves part of Churches that no longer recognised the authority of Lambeth Palace. Socially conservative and primarily evangelical, the new wing – calling itself anything from Renewed Anglican to Refined Evangelical – claimed to want nothing to do with those whom it saw as distorting Scripture.

However, the split was less dramatic than might appear. While it drew a social and theological line between believers on just a handful of issues, within a generation the appetite for a fight on homosexuality was simply no longer there. It may have taken longer to heal the wounds than it did for them to be inflicted, but heal they did. Just as communication technology divided, so too did it help to unite the

2016
H5N1 mutates into HN73

2017
High point of Christian activism on poverty

2017 – 2018
Sub-Saharan Africa devastated by drought

2017 – 2018
Fossil fuel estimates revised significantly downwards

fragmented body of believers. Within a handful of decades the issue of gay Christians appeared as anachronistic as women priests or gentile believers.

CHAOS

While the Church was experiencing the shifting of tectonic plates, becoming more socially active in some parts while experiencing bitter division in others, there were other transitions lining up that were to prove beyond its control. In its infancy, the twenty-first century was widely heralded as the 'make or break' century. Commentators and futurists were convinced that the following hundred years would either become the earth's final days or the beginning of a whole new phase of history. While every generation falls for the same kind of arrogance and believes in the imminence of apocalypse, the claims made at the start of the third millennium were a little more substantial than those suffering from Bubonic plague in the fourteenth century or those who anticipated Christ's return in 1843 (or 1844 for that matter).

Something was different in the early 2000s. It wasn't just the power of the early atomic bomb – nuclear weapons had offered the opportunity to annihilate all life on the planet since the 1960s (a fact about which the Church had been curiously silent). Lining up against humanity were a bewildering array of foes: ultra-rapid population growth, unstoppable climate change, mass depletion of ocean stocks, desertification and widespread soil erosion, increase in drought-related famine, the rise of non-state groups with access to ultimate weapons, religious fundamentalism and terrorism, extreme poverty,

2001
Terrorist attacks on USA

2008 – 2011
Depression 2.0

2013
Increased terrorist activity begins

2014
Anglican Communion split

economic collapse and raging pandemics. Few of these threats on their own held the power to fully annihilate the 6 billion population, but a combination of two or more could overwhelm entirely.

Such was the state of the world that the shifts in Church culture were ultimately insufficient. At first many were reluctant to admit it, preferring instead to see the continued growth as a sign of genuine success. The Second Reformation movement epitomised this, drawing together evangelicals, Unitarians, Catholics and many Pentecostals (both in number from the developing world) to fight the twin issues of extreme poverty and climate change. While the first Reformation had changed the way the Church conducted its internal affairs, their claims for the Second Reformation pointed to the way in which the Church responded to the injustices beyond its doors.

The rhetoric was powerful and their numbers grew. They even made a dent in the egregious state of global poverty, injecting vast sums of money into micro-finance and basic healthcare projects. The poorest communities in Asia and sub-Saharan Africa – particularly Cambodia, Burundi and Angola – found themselves transformed. A network of local churches, west, east and south emerged, and by the middle of 2017 the results from the latest United Nations Panel on Global Poverty Reduction were heralded as the ultimate evidence that Christianity had returned to the heights of the nineteenth-century social activists.

The good news was short lived. Internal disagreement over action versus evangelism grew. Some groups pushed hard for conversion, others did not. While Christian Liberalism had all but died with the

2016
H5N1 mutates into HN73

2017
High point of Christian activism on poverty

2017 – 2018
Sub-Saharan Africa devastated by drought

2017 – 2018
Fossil fuel estimates revised significantly downwards

Anglican split, the Second Reformation found itself re-enacting similar battles between liberal and evangelical from previous centuries.

These internal struggles needn't have caused much harm by themselves. What damaged Christianity almost beyond repair were events far beyond their control.

THE THREE HORRORS

Attacks on western targets by Islamic fundamentalists had been a familiar news story since the 1996 *fatwah* issued by Osama bin Laden. New York, Madrid, London, Copenhagen and Nairobi had all been sites of major terrorist attacks by the time 2012 ended. Yet it was at that point that their frequency and intensity began to increase. One by one most developed western nations experienced their own tragedies at the hands of the Al-Qaeda network. The proliferation of home-made explosive devices strapped to suicide bombers claimed significantly greater numbers of lives than all the previous attacks combined. Instead of targeting high-profile buildings or events, the bombers turned to the Troubles of North Ireland during the latter part of the previous century for inspiration. Chaos and carnage were the key objectives, and from 2013 onwards barely a month went by without news of another western urban area dominated by broken glass and bodybags.

The second development was initially more subtle, yet far more lethal. It was flu. HN51 had brooded on the horizon since 2003, threatening to make the major jump from chickens to humans with no promise of a cure. Numbers of annual fatalities had never climbed

2001
Terrorist attacks on USA

2008 – 2011
Depression 2.0

2013
Increased terrorist activity begins

2014
Anglican Communion split

higher than 150, yet in 2016 the graph turned sharply up. HN51 mutated into HN73, a form affecting humans with devastating lethality. Before a vaccine could be created it had spread from its original site in Mexico City, through North and South America and across to Europe, Africa and Asia. In densely populated areas it claimed as much as fifteen per cent of local populations. Within seventeen months it had killed more than eleven million people (including 750,000 in the USA, 400,000 in the UK and three million across South America).

Finally, while the world's markets recovered from Depression 2.0 (2008–2011), the early optimism as the downturn was declared complete soon gave way to panic. Oil, coal and gas reserves had been grossly over estimated, and while it eventually forced the Global Clean Energy Act, governments were at that point wholly unprepared for the change required. As renewable energy was drastically rationed across the developed world – and the use of fossil fuels reserved by most governments for their own humanitarian work in the fight against HN73 – manufacturing and transport all but expired. Economies that once boomed were silenced. Global poverty became no respecter of international border or status and those who had known extreme poverty in the years before were suddenly unplugged from whatever lifeline humanitarian aid was offering them. Across sub-Saharan Africa in particular, the famines of 2017 and 2018 left millions starved and dead.

Like the so-called Great War a century before, the combination of economic collapse, pandemic and terrorism changed the world drastically. Known as the Three Horrors, they were responsible for

2016
H5N1 mutates into HN73

2017
High point of Christian activism on poverty

2017 – 2018
Sub-Saharan Africa devastated by drought

2017 – 2018
Fossil fuel estimates revised significantly downwards

the death of up to 23 million people. Old assumptions and previously held values were yet again jettisoned in the hope that without their weight the balloon might just begin to climb once more. Capitalism and its companion, consumerism – for so long a curious blend of hobby, religion and political system – was the first to go. So too did the north/south divide and the status of the USA as lone superpower. Faith too was battered. People became increasingly suspicious of major religions, and Christianity was no exception. Too many people had been promised healing from HN73 by the self-professed Healing Apostles who spread across the evangelical Church or the followers of the Saints who emerged from the Catholic Church. The Christian answers to terrorism had been flimsy at best – ranging from re-establishing the Crusades to the practise of *portable communion* (daily confession, absolution and the Eucharist via video call for a small monthly subscription fee).

As for the economic crisis, the Green Church were at last taken seriously, yet a small number of believers took the depletion of the earth's resources as a sign of the imminent return of Christ and opted to ignore the initial energy consumption restrictions. Prosecution and house detainment soon cut their numbers down.

And what of the fight against global poverty? Did the success spread from Cambodia, Burundi and Angola? Did the Church at least remember to check in on those whose lives they had saved when their own were not under threat? Did the support continue in spite of the hardship at home?

It did not.

Chapter Fourteen

2020 – 2062
The Age of Endings

In the end, there was little fuss. The outcries were muted and the protests short lived. There was coverage across the international media, but it was only cursory. Even the attempts to boost reception figures by labelling it The Death of Christendom failed to truly capture the imagination. The plain fact was as simple as it was stark; few in the west cared that Christianity had finally lost its claim as the ruling theology across Europe and the United States of America.

It happened with a pen stroke, and the anachronism seemed fitting. Throughout the 2050s and 2060s leaders of the word's last *Christian nations* had all, to some degree, put greater distance between state and Church. In Great Britain it took the form of King William VI formally rescinding his claim as Head of what was left of the Anglican Church, while in Spain an act of the *Cortes Generales* put an end to the country's brief experiment of closer alignment with the Catholic Church that had started in 2048. America had less far to travel, but the 41st amendment to the constitution in 2057 made clear that the ground had shifted by removing the word 'God' from the Pledge of Allegiance and the national motto.

These were all significant, but lacked the flourish of the pen held by Pope Leo XIV on 4 January 2063. His signature brought to an end the State of the Vatican City, returning the 110 acres to Italian sovereignty, albeit with a clear understanding that the Holy See would remain the home of the Roman Catholic Church. Unable to effectively defend itself from both terrorist attack and looming environmental catastrophe, the Catholic Church was forced to go begging to the Italian state. At any other time during the previous two centuries it would have inconceivable to imagine Italy offering

2029
Collapse of Soviet State

2033
Utah becomes Independent Republic of the Latter Day Saints

2035
Scientists synthesize Telomerase

2037 – 2040
Golan Heights/al-Jawlān return to Syria

anything other than total submission and full support to the Holy Father. Yet changing times had left the government in a different position. The power was their own now, and in spite of sporadic protests, the handover was considered a reasonable price to pay.

WHITE NOISE AND BLURRED LINES

Change, as we know, gathers its own pace. It increases until it becomes unstoppable, driven by a momentum that continues regardless of attempts to halt or reverse it. Of course not all change reaches the event horizon – the point beyond which an object is unable to resist the gravitational pull of a black hole – but in the days of the mid-twenty-first century, society appeared oblivious as all around change hurled the world against the wall.

It used to be that shifts in culture occurred every couple of centuries; that life-changing inventions like spinning wheels and electric lights appeared only when previous generations had died and their tombstones began to fade. Not now. After the chaos storms of 2013 to 2017 – when terrorism, pandemics and fuel-poverty brought many societies to their knees - it was obvious that transformation was arriving with every passing decade.

If it was difficult to determine the particular sound that defined such change, it was not because the changes lacked focus or resisted such definition. It was because there was too much white noise in the background to single out any individual theme. World religions clashed and raged against themselves and each other, technological advances promised both hope and terror, the planet was plagued by both flood and drought and populations both exploded and imploded. From each

2041
Schism in Catholic Church

2043
Southern Ocean declared toxic

2057
'God' removed from American Pledge of Allegiance

2058
Greater Miami abandoned to flood waters

region and each issue came a philosophy for managing the change, and the Church was not alone in attempting to offer leadership out of the wilderness. The trouble was, the western flock had scattered long ago.

During the 2020s the Slow Faith movement had more success than many other Christian groups. Having witnessed the evolution of other *Slow*... movements (food, transport and education) it was inevitable that some in the Church would follow suit. Just as the foodies shunned the pre-prepared, instant meals, and the transporters eased off on the throttle and the schoolers scaled back the testing, so the Slow Church took a series of steps back from what it saw as detrimental influences around it. With the emphasis on a return to meditation the group drew from the Quakers and early monastic communities, while its preference for liturgy and connections with the history of Christianity as a whole brought it into closer contact with the Orthodox Church. However, the focus on environmental care and emphasis on lifestyle over doctrine limited their appeal in the evangelical growth areas across Africa.

While Pentecostalism had continued to grow, all around its cousins were in decline. Apart from the Mormons, that is. In a bizarre turn that flew in the face of the predicted and well-chronicled decline in church attendance, The Church of Jesus Christ of Latter Day Saints found itself one of the dominant religious voices within America. While few had been looking it had amassed significant wealth and gained tangible political power within its adopted home state of Utah. In 2033 it staged an audacious – and successful –- secession bid, forming the independent Republic of the Latter Day Saints. It legalised polygamy, withdrew the right to vote from women and turned back the clock by almost 200 years. The population grew

2029
Collapse of Soviet State

2033
Utah becomes Independent Republic of the Latter Day Saints

2035
Scientists synthesize Telomerase

2037 – 2040
Golan Heights/al-Jawlān return to Syria

to twenty-five million and the Republic was admitted to the United Nations. That, it seemed was enough, or at least, it was as good as it was to get for the Church. In spite of talk of it as the Mormon Vatican and discovery of lost prophesies from founder Joseph Smith that claimed it would become the dominant Christian denomination by the time 2050 rolled around, the secession of 2033 was the summit of its climb rather than the base camp. Mormonism experienced a slight resurgence among other western cultures, but the move towards legalised misogyny placed a definite limit on its appeal.

The real change came from the east. With 100 PhD students in China for every one student working on their doctorate in America, it was clear even at the start of the century that the balance of power within the world was about to be significantly altered. What only a few predicted, however, was the fact that Christianity would for the first time in seventeen hundred years lose its claim to political power. Christendom was gone and faith in Jesus Christ returned once more to the underground.

THE MAP

The years 2013-2017 left the world shocked and shattered. Like the Great War a century before, it left people with torn-down assumptions about the essence of their security. While the Church had largely failed to take full advantage of this situation in the 1920s, the same could not be said in the 2020s. From three distinct directions the Church struggled to claw back its place in society. To say each failed would be overly simplistic, and while the hoped-for resuscitation of the struggling patient failed to arrive, the efforts of the period were not in vain.

2041
Schism in Catholic Church

2043
Southern Ocean declared toxic

2057
'God' removed from American Pledge of Allegiance

2058
Greater Miami abandoned to flood waters

First the Catholic Church stepped up its rhetoric and represented itself as a source of authority and security in troubled times. Pope Benedict XVI had established himself as a force for conservatism since his investment in 2005, refusing to even tinker with the Catholic position on contraception from the outset and bemoaning the decline in Christian values among European nations at the time. His twelve-year term in office paved the way for Cardinal Pietro Vittorelli, former Abbot of Montecassino, to become Pope Gregory XVII and bring with him an authoritarian voice that had not been heard from the Holy See for some time.

The state of the world, claimed the new Pope during his investiture, was a clear indication of divine judgment. Speaking on the eve of the first United Nations Global Energy Summit in 2017, he declared the Three Horrors to be punishment for the very godlessness that his predecessor had raged against. 'God never promised to meet us in the shops,' he thundered. 'And we must leave our toys outside the Church.'

His words struck a chord with some, and over the following thirty-two years he became increasingly focused on the core message; society must repent if things were to get better. Contraception, abortion, female ordination; all issues which some may have hoped the Church would shift on, retreated to the most conservative corners of the argument, with wildly different results around the world.

In China, Catholicism experienced something of a resurgence. Since Benedict's Papacy there had been a slow thawing of relations, and with Gregory XVII's criticism of ideologies previously held dear by so many in the west – particularly consumerism, liberalism and pluralism – he appealed to the authority's sense of vanity.

2029
Collapse of Soviet State

2033
Utah becomes Independent Republic of the Latter Day Saints

2035
Scientists synthesize Telomerase

2037 – 2040
Golan Heights/al-Jawlān return to Syria

South America was relatively receptive, up to a point. Catholicism there had long been aware of the need for social transformation, although while Rome espoused the value of behavioural shift, those in Latin America understood the need to be in continued reform of political structures. With the Amazon fires of 2041, relations with Rome deteriorated. Years of rising temperatures had turned much of the land into little more than tinder that yielded itself to the flames at the slightest touch. In six months over 30 per cent of the forest was destroyed, taking with it the lives of millions living in shantycities on the edge of La Paz and Iquitos. Two million people died in the blazes and the disease that followed. When the Catholic Churches and diocese looked to Rome for support, little support came back. The anger that followed was palpable and played a significant factor, as did the sense for many that the political structure that was now in most need of reform was not their own government, but the core of their Church. The inevitable split that followed was the first schism within the Catholic Church since the days of Luther and Henry VIII. The shock dulled considerably this second time around.

Meanwhile, in Europe the number of Catholics in relation to Protestants grew. Evangelicalism was struggling, and Gregory's words offered the lure of strong leadership. While the exodus of peripheral Christians away from the Church had been going on for some time, those who remained members of European Churches, regardless of denomination, were part of the core faithful, a minority but one that was not going to leave. However, as we shall see later, evangelicalism's glue was starting to lose strength, and the transfer to Roman Catholic allegiance was becoming increasingly common.

If Europe was its success, then it was in Africa that Catholicism suffered

2041
Schism in Catholic Church

2043
Southern Ocean declared toxic

2057
'God' removed from American Pledge of Allegiance

2058
Greater Miami abandoned to flood waters

its greatest defeat. The population of sub-Saharan Africa had grown with incredible speed. Uganda, Burkina Faso and Congo, for example, all quadrupled their population within the first half of the century, and the continent's overall population went from a little under 1 billion in 2000 to 3.6 billion in 2050. The population boom put incredible pressure on already scarce resources, increased the outbreak of civil war in those countries that appeared addicted to violent discord, and left political and civil leaders with one message on their lips; humanity must control the population before nature does. Unwilling to reverse its opposition to contraception, the Catholic Church was hammered. African leaders were outraged, particularly when the Church refused to increase aid. Starved of support and unable to offer the essentials that people needed, bit by bit the Church watched itself disappear.

Strangely, the dramatic growth in India's population did not have similar results. When, on 17 June 2051 India officially became the world's largest nation (1.75 billion people as opposed to China's 1.4 billion), the country celebrated with fireworks and speeches. There was little need for contraception that night.

THE SCREEN

Europe's numbers were falling. First it was Spain, Greece and Germany that struggled, then Russia, Romania and Bulgaria saw their populations decline. While this had serious consequences for their economies, the ageing population had little effect in the Church. What did change was the typical reaction to the legacy of global instability.

Of the Three Horrors, it was terrorism that had initially prompted governments to act. Surveillance increased, particularly that made

2029
Collapse of Soviet State

2033
Utah becomes Independent Republic of the Latter Day Saints

2035
Scientists synthesize Telomerase

2037 – 2040
Golan Heights/al-Jawlān return to Syria

possible by advances in nanotechnology. Drones could fly unmanned and undetected while tracking individuals. Undetectably small transmitters also allowed tracking to be carried efficiently, while DNA scanning and computer processing technology advanced dramatically enough to allow a central European database to monitor, in real time, the movement of forty per cent of the population within its borders. So long as people breathed while they passed beneath the scanners, their presence was mapped.

Many of those Churches that had previously embraced new Christian social activism now had a new cause to support; the fight against the invasion of privacy. Not that they were against catching terrorists, but they knew their Orwell and Atwood well enough to spot the beginnings of a sharp decline when they saw one. While poverty had been one of the main concerns of many in the Church during the 2000s and early twenty-teens, the twenties were host to battles against the state. The Libertarian Evangelicals underestimated not just their opponents but their potential supporters too. While the governments ignored their protests and carried on regardless, the rest of the population had little sympathy for the cause. In a world turned brutally unsafe, Big Government was the solution that many in Europe and the USA wanted. What happened to the few that were left among the assorted Libertarian Evangelical faithful was obvious; their numbers contracted a little, year by year, until there was not much more than a trace left of their existence. They had never favoured ostentatious church buildings or even put too much emphasis on the importance of meetings in general. For many congregations they simply moved down the rental list, using ever-smaller properties for their Sunday meetings, until there was barely any sign of them at all.

2041
Schism in Catholic Church

2043
Southern Ocean declared toxic

2057
'God' removed from American Pledge of Allegiance

2058
Greater Miami abandoned to flood waters

While the Catholic Church headed off in the direction of austere leadership and the Libertarian Evangelicals tried but failed to rally the secular masses, the core of Evangelical Christianity also refused to stay silent. The rise of global terrorism had given some cause to champion the return of the Religious Right, though in truth it would be fairer to say that this was a new phenomenon rather than a rehash of a previous one. Still, there were similarities; an aggressive foreign policy was adopted by some, and Israel's future in an increasingly hostile region was deemed to be of primary importance.

The commercialism of the late-twentieth century re-emerged in the wake of the Three Horrors, having been silenced only a little by the intervening years. Instead of televangelists urging hefty donations, there emerged a new breed of 'ministry'; the so called *apocalyptic accountants*. Using the age-old technique adopted by weary parents everywhere, Churches thundered beneath the threat of annihilation, judgement and eternal damnation. In the most extreme cases people were subject to graphic descriptions of what would happen to them in hell, and *rapture-readiness* emerged as a billion dollar industry. Between the two you could arrive at a Church network site, enter the details of your sins, have yourself scanned and watch a life-size animation of your eternal punishment. Once finished it was possible – for a small fee – to put your life back on track and keep it there thanks to the multi-pronged approach of those aiming to maintain your state of personal readiness for Christ's return and your exit up to heaven.

Not everyone fell for it, but much of the rest of the evangelical Church found themselves lost in the world. They retreated to what they knew to be truth; the authority of Scripture and the leadership of those in front of the camera. Teaching in Biblical prophecy increased in popularity, while many Churches reworked the prosperity gospel with a new twist; if you had faith enough, not only would you be prosperous in health and wealth, but the faithful Christians would know themselves assured of their place in heaven. A simple circle was created; if salvation came through faith alone, and faith was rewarded with blessings (or a financial and physical variety), then surely those who were wealthy were assured of their salvation? And because wealth was proved in many ways – with not everyone choosing to flaunt it in these dangerous times – the only true way of proving yourself was by giving over a certain amount to the Church.

Just like the selling of indulgences by Pope Leo X, the sales of faith caused outrage. Yet where was the modern day Martin Luther? Who would damn the Church and nail the accusations to the church door?

By now the world beyond the Church had ceased to truly care. There were other, far more pressing concerns to tackle.

In 2054 the speculation about runaway climate change was almost put to rest. A series of dramatic events and catastrophes combined to prove, almost beyond doubt, that the planet was rejecting human life once and for all. At first it was the sea; stocks of fish, which had already been falling throughout the century, finally all but disappeared. The levels of acidity in the oceans increased, and the bulk of the Southern Ocean had been declared toxic in 2043. Unable to support basic organisms, the entire food chain was disrupted. Within five years global fish stock had fallen by 83 per cent, leaving entire communities with no means of sustaining their livelihoods.

Then it was the ice. As global temperatures rose, the Siberian,

2041
Schism in Catholic Church

2043
Southern Ocean declared toxic

2057
'God' removed from American Pledge of Allegiance

2058
Greater Miami abandoned to flood waters

Alaskan, Canadian and Greenland icecaps and permafrost melted. Releasing billions of tonnes of carbon that had been stored in the frozen soil – as well as methane from freshly active bacteria - global warming accelerated beyond all but the most pessimistic models.

The Amazon fires of 2041 released yet more carbon into the atmosphere, and the rise in global temperatures threatened to reverse the carbon cycle, with vegetation and soils no longer storing carbon but releasing it.

Then the seas rose. As early as 2005 there was talk of evacuating the Polynesian island of Tuvalu, and by 2050 it was fully submerged. The Nile Delta, the Netherlands, Bangladesh, Vietnam and in the USA almost every east coast city from Boston to Miami was swamped. Several Caribbean islands were engulfed, while the Maldives and Marshall Islands vanished.

Of course, in the wealthy countries these cities and regions had long since been abandoned, but in the east and south, 50 million people each year were victims of the race to avoid the waters that rose.

The Church was in a unique position. For some it was a vindication, a Biblical apocalypse to drive the people back towards the Bible. It worked for some, and the trend towards an old Catholic east and new Catholic South America continued. But few were attracted to the rhetoric employed by many in the evangelical wing of the Church. While the new Pope Paul VII (the first pope from China) led mass repentance and encouraged a reconnection with the Christian role of steward of the earth, what remained of the publicly visible Church in the west still refused to acknowledge that the catastrophes were primarily a result of human mismanagement. This was the end of the age, they declared. Jesus was coming back soon.

Chapter Fifteen

2049 – 2098
The Rise of the Tiger Theology

Far from heralding the return of the Son of God and the end of life on earth for the true believers, the turmoil was the precursor to a different sort of finale; the end of the evangelical Church as a global concern.

Of course, it had been coming for years. The collapse of Christendom had been one of the final blows from which it was unable to recover, and the closed ears and eyes to the cries of the planet were another example of institutional suicide. But it was the 43 day war of winter 2062 that consigned the three hundred year history of evangelicalism to the museum of Christian past.

Not that the entire movement lacked significance or influence; not, for example, like the pornocracy (a sixty year period at the start of the tenth century when the ruling popes were themselves controlled by a family of influential courtesans) or the time when Taiwanese priest Joseph Lv married a pair of (heterosexual) pigs. No, the evangelical movement had been hugely significant and influential, but it was about to expire.

The war started, like so many before in the region, with water. Summer droughts were nothing new of course, but the autumn of 2062 was unusually hot in Israel. As ever, residents in al-Jawl n (or the Golan Heights as the area was known before Israel handed it over to Syria following the 2037–2040 war) were attempting to increase yield from hydro-electric plants beneath the Sea of Galilee, two miles from the Syrian coast on the west. When an explosion within the main plant occurred – killing five workers and injuring fourteen – and evidence of foul play emerged, attention turned to neighbouring Israel. Eventually the Likud Freedom Movement claimed responsi-

2051
Significant minority of Chinese population claim to be Christian

2062
Nuclear attack on Israel kills 9 million

2063
Vatican loses independent status

2070s
Evangelical churches decline

bility. Within days the incident became an outcry, then a standoff and eventually a full-scale conflict, with guerrilla forces attacking homes in al-Jawl n, and members of the Syrian Defence Force responding with military drone attacks on Israeli defence positions.

The conflict continued as so many had before; civilian and military casualties mounting, individuals in Israel retreating to their communal bunkers whenever surveillance managed to track the drones in Israeli airspace, residents in al-Jawl n relying on good fortune and hope in their efforts to avoid the roaming LFM fighters. Eventually, so the assumption went, the house of Saud would intervene and send everyone home.

Not this time. On 16 December Ahmed Kiir and Salva al-Mufti boarded a microjet in Jabal Qadir, southern Sudan and flew to Amman, Jordan. The next day they arrived in Palestine, although how they got there is not clear. What is known is that, having crawled through long-abandoned smugglers' tunnels left over from the West Bank occupation, at 8:12am Kiir and al-Mufti were able to detonate two micro-hydrogen bombs half a mile from the centre of Jerusalem. Each with a fifteen kiloton yield, the blast radius levelled all buildings within a twenty mile radius.

Simultaneous explosions in Nazareth, Beersheba and Tel Aviv instantly killed 9 million people, seventy-five per cent of Israel's population at the time. Fatalities in Palestine were equally high. As the thousand kilometre per hour winds were followed by epic firestorms, Israel – one of the youngest nations on earth – was ripped from its face. Neighbouring Palestine, also young, also home to an unwanted tribe of ancient nomads, was similarly annihilated.

2090s
Emergence of 'Tiger Theology'

2090s
Water wars, Africa

2091
Bolivia, Chile, Brazil and Suriname leave United Nations

2093
Malaria claims 13 million lives

What followed has been well documented. Around 90% of the population of both Israel and Palestine died, either directly in the blast or as a result of radiation poisoning. Of the 1 million Israeli citizens left, tens of thousands were caught and held in quarantine zones, while the bulk of those few that survived took shelter in India. Prime Minister Wassim, urged by an alliance of Church and civic leaders, took the initiative in offering the refugees a home. There was little romance in the relocation, no stories from the ancient scrolls to attach to modern maps. India was strange land and once more they were strangers in it. Yet, overcrowded as it was and broken by shock and trauma as many of the Israelis were, the offer of kindness from strangers won them over, and within months India's resources were under a little more strain, but the country's international standing was second to none.

There were no retaliations, no second strike. Sudan's long internal battles with Islamic extremism and Al-Qaeda had been well followed, and there was little need to look beyond the network of terror cells for the guilty party. Others tried, of course, and the Syrian government was called on to defend itself. Eventually, the decimation of Palestine was enough evidence to delete blame from any other Middle East nation.

As the radiation caused health problems across the region for decades, the death of Israel and Palestine forced the rules of international politics to be rewritten. First, the various nations, kingdoms and states of the Middle East closed ranks. Quarantine zones were the start of this, but a genuine mistrust of the world outside the region fuelled it. The area became a closed shop, and the so-called Iron

2051
Significant minority of Chinese population claim to be Christian

2062
Nuclear attack on Israel kills 9 million

2063
Vatican loses independent status

2070s
Evangelical churches decline

Tapestry went up. A sort of harmony descended, but one mixed with fear, death and sorrow. While Islam grieves in public, it could only rebuild its family in private.

The former powers of America and Europe were impotent. There was talk of retaliation and reprisals, but when India stepped in as shepherd, nurse and protector of the remaining Israelis, the former world leaders breathed a sigh of relief. Much as the Middle East did, the once-wealthy and utterly dominant west retreated. International borders were increasingly fortified and crossing over them became ever more difficult. Surveillance increased, many foreign nationals were expelled and everyone hoped that this was an incident that would never be repeated.

THE SKIES

Rome and Santiago were both silent. What could the Catholic Church do? While the tensions had been escalating there had been little to say – this appeared to be business as usual for the region. But once the blasts had been released from their bombs, there was little to do but pray.

To the evangelicals, however, this was not merely a call to prayer. It was the very apocalypse itself. For weeks before large numbers of preachers had been pointing to the region and cross-referencing events with Daniel's apocalyptic undertones. Such was the level of anticipation that many Christians had stopped working during the early days of December, getting rapture-ready with top-ups to their Church tithe accounts and attending gatherings where the latest events were decoded and plotted on a real-time countdown calendar.

2090s
Emergence of 'Tiger Theology'

2090s
Water wars, Africa

2091
Bolivia, Chile, Brazil and Suriname leave United Nations

2093
Malaria claims 13 million lives

As news of the blasts spread like aftershocks, millions of Christians in the UK, the USA, Germany and Norway were already at church. Replays of the towering mushroom clouds over the flattened Holy City were greeted with prayers, songs, cries of 'hallelujah', even cheers. Eyes searched the skies for parting clouds or shafts of light. The end was nigh, surely? Wasn't this it?

RAPTURE GRIEF

A year later and the membership numbers of evangelical Churches were falling. Public broadcasting of sermons, meetings and merchandise opportunities ceased, in some states due to government control, in others due simply to a lack of interest. Evangelicalism imploded, and within a decade the movement had been reduced to a collection of isolated churches and networks based around urban developments or – for those who had got out with enough money – in Church-administered communities. Their surveillance, walls and gates were sharper and higher than those on other urban developments, and as the term 'evangelical' slipped from common use, those that remained faithful to the values it had evolved into became known as the Hidden Church.

Those living behind the gates faced a unique set of challenges. Like the early settlers in North America they were faced with the challenge of building a life from nothing, although the late-twenty-first century version of such poverty hardly matched the Pilgrim Fathers' hardship. With enough money behind them the Hidden Church communities were self-sufficient in nearly every respect. Hydroponics and nutritional fungal tanks took care of the food –

2051
Significant minority of Chinese population claim to be Christian

2062
Nuclear attack on Israel kills 9 million

2063
Vatican loses independent status

2070s
Evangelical churches decline

and the convenient conversion to the vegetarianism that the Catholic and Slow Faith Churches had been promoting for years ensured that what little land they had could be used to maximum effect. The fact the Hidden Church communities occupied land in hilly areas kept them free from the risks of rising sea levels, and solar, hydro and wind power were all utilised with maximum efficiency. Ironically, for a group that had cared little about the planet for decades, they became remarkably adept at ensuring that they used what resources the earth was lending them with the greatest of care.

Many of those who parted ways with the Church at this point found themselves unsure of what to make of the events. Rapture grief became a common topic of conversation, and while some followed the flow over to the Catholic Church, others simply abandoned the institution altogether. They looked back with wry envy to the days of their grandparents, when secularism ruled and religion could be a part time social interest and little else. Having come close to destruction – if not heaven itself – the luxury of such denial was something people could ill-afford.

THE RISING SUN

It was from the east that help for many came. The century had been good to both India and China, as well as, to a lesser extent, Thailand and Korea, leading to much talk about the influence of the Tiger Economy. Asia was now clearly dominant in terms of the global market place, and for years innovation had poured out from the laboratories of Chennai, Hyderabad, Nanjing, Xi'an and Guangzhou. The cities became to technology what Florence was to art in the

2090s
Emergence of 'Tiger Theology'

2090s
Water wars, Africa

2091
Bolivia, Chile, Brazil and Suriname leave United Nations

2093
Malaria claims 13 million lives

sixteenth century or what America was to business in the twentieth.

China and India were beginning to dominate the Church as well, and the Tiger Theology began to emerge. The improvement in relations with Catholicism had seen an increase in the Church as a result, but it was the indigenous Church in each country that truly thrived. The numbers themselves explain much of the story, with sixty per cent of Chinese declaring themselves Christians at the end of the twenty-first century. Numbers were slightly lower in India, but thanks to a remarkable event in Haridwar, all that was about to change.

Haridwar had never played much more than the smallest of bit-parts in Christianity's story. One of the seven holiest Hindu cities, it only ever had vague associations with the Church – the occasional priest or missionary from the nineteenth century onwards, perhaps a house-church or two throughout the decades of the twentieth century. But not now. Today Haridwar is irreversibly linked with Christians, martyrs and miracles.

The story starts in 2103. Buoyed by its regaining of the entire Kashmir region – helped, in large part by it forgiving beleaguered neighbour Pakistan in excess of $Rs.82 trillion of unpaid debt – India's Christian Socialist Party decided to tackle the second of the country's twin headaches: the tensions between Christian and Hindu in the country's poorer northern states.

Despite intense media satellite surveillance and observations the facts remain a little hazy at best. We know that on the morning of 3 June 2103 a group of Christians from the Haridwar Apostolic Centre conducted their typical weekly activities in the town, delivering food to a local orphanage and holding prayer meetings in the main street.

2051
Significant minority of Chinese population claim to be Christian

2062
Nuclear attack on Israel kills 9 million

2063
Vatican loses independent status

2070s
Evangelical churches decline

Nothing particularly unusual about the activities, apart from the fact that they were filmed, commentated on and broadcast live by three members of the Hindu militia group, Shiv Sena – originally formed in 1966 as a far right political party dedicated to the cause Hindu nationalism, but long since having devolved into a family of insurgents and militants.

Describing the Christians as 'vile' and 'parasites' the leader of the group went on to explain his intentions: to follow the eight back to their vehicle (parked behind a deserted school), beat them, force them to recant their faith or face immediate execution. This, he claimed, would finally show the world quite how weak were God's followers.

It happened as predicted, although the Christians failed to follow their part of the script. When told to denounce their faith, they did not. In turn they were clearly seen to look at each other, then up at the lead militia, stating 'I believe Jesus is the son of God, crucified, died and buried, rose again to new life.' The pause that followed was eventually punctuated by the sound of multiple gunshots. In turn the Christians – clearly dead – crumpled to the ground, as though the earth's gravity beneath them had momentarily quadrupled.

By this time several news broadcasters had connected to the story and their overhead surveillance feeds took over the narration. Viewers saw the police arrive and a standoff begin. It ended with one of the militia -– Malik Dhara – shot dead at 10:04 and the other two caught and arrested.

Seventeen minutes passed, and at 10:21 paramedics arrived and declared the Christians dead. So too, eventually was Dhara pronounced dead. Loaded onto a gurney, his body was set to one side while police

2090s
Emergence of 'Tiger Theology'

2090s
Water wars, Africa

2091
Bolivia, Chile, Brazil and Suriname leave United Nations

2093
Malaria claims 13 million lives

carried out initial forensic investigations and the eight victims were loaded into the ambulances. As the overhead zoomed in to get a clearer picture, Dhara's face could clearly be seen: eyes fixed ahead, skin pallid, face rigid. Several of the news broadcasters started to transmit archive footage of his previous activities until, at 10:59 something changed. Dhara started to twitch, his eyes blinked and within seconds he was clearly conscious again, tears mingling with the dried blood around his left temple, his breathing increasingly rapid and deep. Eventually a medic caught sight of the change and moved in to investigate. Malik Dhara – militant Hindu activist – was alive after all, back from the dead. So much for reincarnation.

While there are many cases throughout history of individuals having near (or actual) death experiences, none had been documented by a real-time broadcast. The fallout was therefore immense. Months later Malik has traded infamy for fame, speaking hesitantly about the 55 minutes during which he was officially dead, but eloquently about his newfound faith in Christ to countless journalists and news presenters. As for what happened during the hour he was dead, opinion was divided. A few suspected a conspiracy, many more sceptics simply claimed that it could not be true though they could not prove why. But for millions Dhara's transformation from militant Hindu to Christian apologist was one that they were simply unable to ignore.

MALARIAL MISSIONS

India had proved it was serious about its new role as a global leader in the weeks and months after the destruction of Israel and Palestine.

2051
Significant minority of Chinese population claim to be Christian

2062
Nuclear attack on Israel kills 9 million

2063
Vatican loses independent status

2070s
Evangelical churches decline

A second challenge emerged as the twenty-first century drew to a close. Water wars had been predicted for a long time, and fighting had broken out among many sub-Saharan countries over increasingly scarce resources. What changed, however, was the increasing pressure of internal competition.

The Saharan Solar Project had transformed the region around the desert. Over a billion solar panels and parabolic mirrors had been installed above the sands, creating enough electricity to bring significant wealth and power to the countries fortunate enough to own a piece of the desert. While those to the north and east (among them Morocco, Libya, Egypt and Sudan) were able to enjoy their increased wealth without much opposition, those countries to the south (Niger, Mali and Chad) were under constant threat from southern neighbours.

War over water erupted throughout the 2090s, with southern African countries launching frequent attacks on their northern cousins. Retaliation from well-funded armies followed, and while many southern counties had no armies with which to defend themselves (only to attack), the fighting continued. Mass migration around southern Africa followed, and people became increasingly desperate. Malaria – a disease many had thought had been eradicated with the global vaccination programme of 2026–2027, returned. Once again the phrase 'death by mosquito bite' became a chilling indictment of a world divided between those with money and those without. In 2093 alone malaria claimed the lives of 13 million adults across sub-Saharan Africa.

It was the Church that stepped in and helped. Fearful of a re-run

2090s
Emergence of 'Tiger Theology'

2090s
Water wars, Africa

2091
Bolivia, Chile, Brazil and Suriname leave United Nations

2093
Malaria claims 13 million lives

of the worst parts of the previous two centuries, the Chinese and Indian governments dramatically increased aid to the region. Desalination plants were built, vast hydro-farms built and urban camps established for the millions under threat. Back home, the Church was reluctant to claim victory in either country, but there was no doubt whose voices had been ringing in the ears of the politicians when the Sino-Indian convened to plan emergency action. Demonstrations in Delhi and Beijing had been particularly persuasive, with peaceful protest bringing the cities to a standstill on numerous occasions. The leaders did not need quite so much persuasion, however, as many high ranking officials and cabinet members had marched, sang and prayed alongside the protestors on their way in to the discussions.

Chapter Sixteen

2099 – 2133
Fresh Challenges in a Reworked World

The previous handful of centuries had each been defined to a greater or lesser extent by a central concept. The nineteenth had asked what it meant to be equal, the twentieth wondered what it meant to be powerful, while through the blasts and the floods and the storms the twenty-first asked what it would take to survive. Within each of those centuries the Church played varying roles. It took on the role of chief questioner in the nineteenth, largely vacated the debating chamber during the twentieth and began to offer real solutions during the twenty-first. So were things now looking up?

There is no one-word answer to that question that will do justice to the true picture of the Church in 2100. Yes, there were clear signs of improvement. The rise of numbers and more importantly, impact, of Christians throughout Asia had eased global political tensions and seen the Church tackle social problems with a passion not seen since the abolitionists targeted slavery and the Church took to the Victorian slums. The emergence of the Catholic Church in South America was contentious to some back in Rome, but overall it managed to serve as a focal point for an entire continent.

While rebellions and civil wars over the region's dwindling resources continued to erupt throughout the final years of the twenty-first century, the Church remained an anchor of peace within the area. Occasionally heavy handed and authoritarian, the fortunes had always been a little volatile ever since Francisco Pizarro conquered the Incas in 1532. But Christianity had gradually accepted responsibility for the mess it had created, from cruel dictators to suppression of indigenous cultures. Eventually, an equilibrium was reached, and the continent was guided by the compass of Christian values.

2099
Rapturists announce Year of Departure

2099
Utah University claims 'cure for ageing'

2100
Rapturist attendance declines

2101
International Air-Highways Act

But what of the bad stuff? Any trawl through the list of negatives that blighted the Church at the time must surely include the retreat of the western evangelical Church. The proclamations and predictions about the world's end damaged its standing, but it was both the subsequent hibernation and refusal to reappraise its affections for Biblical Prophecy that did greater harm. While the century started out with evangelicalism as the great hope for the Church, it ended with splintered factions, conspiracy theories and gross denial of history.

The end of Christendom sits in both camps; viewed in the east as a positive wrench of the Church away from the muddied waters of political self-interest, while the remaining western Christians mourned the passing of a period in which their beliefs were not considered fringe or obsolete by default.

But this was past. Society had made it through the twenty-first century test and emerged – like the earth itself – scarred and damaged, but just about intact. What mattered most was the future; how would they cope?

THE CHALLENGE

Something had been going on behind the gates. The LDS (Republic of the Latter Day Saints) had been quiet for some time, and while most suspected that this was merely the Mormon way of keeping things pure, others – particularly in the human science community – had their suspicions.

Longevity, immortality, death-cheats … the terms all point to the crusade to find the key to overcoming the ageing process. So far,

2103
Malik Dhara shot, confirmed dead, comes back to life

2119
Pilgrims to Yarrabah, Australia top 1 million

2128
First manned mission to Mars

2133
Assassination of Joseph Adam Smith III

despite significant advances, that search had failed to find the ultimate solution to the problem of our own mortality. Roberts and Li in 2035 had made the first significant breakthrough with the synthesizing of Telomerase – the enzyme capable of halting DNA breakdown – while 2058's publication of Professor Kim Tae-kook's dubiously titled *Marathon At 112: How I Stayed Young While Getting Old* captured the imagination of millions. But it was not until the scientists at Utah University claimed in 2099 that they had cured ageing completely that the real controversies arose.

There, on screens and in visual hubs for all to see, was their evidence; a perfect family, three generations old, with elegantly greying grandmother, thirty-something mother and docile baby daughter. But it was the two generations of men that caught the attention. The grandfather, arm in arm with his wife, looked no older than his son. Both men looked beyond healthy, as if more than one life was contained within their seemingly immortal bodies. DNA testing proved that Joseph Adam Smith II was in deed the 57-year old father of Joseph Smith III, and the world looked on in amazement.

And so, instantly and without doubt, the twenty-second century found its defining question, before the new year had even begun; what does it mean to be human?

REWIND

Society had had a little time to adapt to the notion of increased longevity. Medical advances had allowed stem cell technology to grow replacement tissue and organs, ending the cruelty of donor-mismatches, organ rejection and the long, slow goodbye of

2099
Rapturists announce Year of Departure

2099
Utah University claims 'cure for ageing'

2100
Rapturist attendance declines

2101
International Air-Highways Act

degenerative illnesses like Alzheimer's and, to a lesser extent, Multiple Sclerosis. Altering the body's decline – so-called 'rusting' – had become not only profitable but largely accepted, despite protests from the Church in the early stages of each advance. Yet until now all the advances had been able to achieve was the delay of the inevitable. Average life expectancy had risen dramatically – from just twenty-two years during the Dark Ages in Britain, up through the mid-thirties during the industrial revolution, towards its peak of 97 in 2099. While Tae-kook had carried on running marathons until a couple of years before his death in 2064, age-related decline was the promised end that awaited all that made it that far.

But the apparent halting of the body's ageing around the mid-thirties was a different matter altogether. Up until this point the controversies had always surrounded the notion of creating life. Now the arguments were about cheating death.

'Death is dead', claimed the LDS Science spokesman, Albert Watts. Invoking Nietzsche, Kant and a whole raft of other ancient philosophers, he claimed that immortality was the new destiny for humanity. Life spans of a thousand years would become a reality. Everything would change. Nothing would remain the same.

This presented the Church – and everyone else – with a problem. How would the planet survive without the term limits of life? Who should be allowed to access the so-called Adam Treatment? If death was over, what did this say about God? Was he no longer needed? Was Christianity – like all other religions that had ever taken root upon the planet – finally dead? Had humanity finally evolved to dispense with faith completely? Were we now gods ourselves?

2103
Malik Dhara shot, confirmed dead, comes back to life

2119
Pilgrims to Yarrabah, Australia top 1 million

2128
First manned mission to Mars

2133
Assassination of Joseph Adam Smith III

Many voices emerged from the Church to slam the developments. The cost to the earth would be far too great, argued many. With resources limited and strict controls already in place upon land and energy use, as well as reproduction in the east and south, there could be no justice in the prospect of a return to a growing population.

Convening for an emergency council in Chile, the Catholic Church, both from Rome and Santiago, slammed the LDS announcements on the grounds that they were an irresponsible act that would lead to population increase. Having been on the wrong end of years of criticism for their opposition to contraception, the cynic might suggest that they knew the arguments were effective. There was no doubting their conviction, and the vehemence with which they criticised the Mormons, pulling out of talks and retreating from previous policies that appeared to show Rome and Utah looking for common ground between their branches of the faith.

Across the USA and northern Europe, there were different reactions. So-called Rapturists saw the advances as an abomination, and yet another sign of the imminent return of Christ. Others who had tethered themselves less tightly to the end-times prophetic movement were a little less hostile. For those members of the Hidden Church living behind their own gates and impenetrable walls, the arguments about the impact on the rest of the world carried little weight. Why not live forever? Sustainable living had become a proven reality in the highground retreats of the Scottish, Norwegian and German hills, and if the individuals who accepted treatment agreed to be sterilised, then why shouldn't they live forever?

2099
Rapturists announce Year of Departure

2099
Utah University claims 'cure for ageing'

2100
Rapturist attendance declines

2101
International Air-Highways Act

The problem, of course, was God. How could they justify cheating death when all along death had been a vital part of Christian life? Without the bridge, would heaven be removed from their horizons?

The Mormons had found a clever way around this. Unearthing previously hidden copies of Joseph Smith's letters, Jethro Hosea – the Church's Principle Theologian at the time – claimed that Smith had foreseen a time when heaven would be available here on earth, without death being involved in the process at all. Smith wrote of the evolution of man into angel, of the new heaven looking very much like the old earth. The Adam Treatment, suggested Hosea, was heaven on earth.

For some Hidden Churchers, this was enough. For the first time since its creation, the Mormon Church expanded beyond the LDS, with twelve communities outside their borders becoming LDS protectorates. Scottish, American, German and Norwegian governments were happy to allow the transfer, particularly when their debts to the LDS were cancelled.

Other Christians accepted the idea of the Adam Treatment, but with less of the Mormon theology attached. However, they soon found that without enough money they were unable to gain any tangible benefit from their support. Left like beggars at the restaurant windows, they went home soon enough.

THE HOUSE CHURCH

We should have got round to the House Church movement by now, but all that technology and terror got in the way. Besides, up until

2103
Malik Dhara shot, confirmed dead, comes back to life

2128
First manned mission to Mars

2119
Pilgrims to Yarrabah, Australia top 1 million

2133
Assassination of Joseph Adam Smith III

now, few thought that they were going anywhere special. It turns out they were wrong, so a history tour is in order.

It started in the late-twentieth century in China. Legal restrictions on public meetings of any kind limited their ability to emulate the Church of Christendom with public worship. The fact that the authorities frequently persecuted the Church and its members had its own unique impact as well, with believers subject to routine harassment, imprisonment and occasional torture.

By the mid-point of the twenty-first century the opposition in China had cooled significantly. Though still communist, the authorities had not only accepted Christianity as a legitimate religion to be more than tolerated, it had adopted many of the values that were deemed appropriate. In a move that would have horrified Karl Marx, Christian Communism rose to become the dominant political force within the state.

Marx may have been horrified, but the Church was not. From the book of Acts to the work of Camilo Torres Restrepo in South American during the twentieth century, communism had more than occasionally connected with Christianity. Were it not for the failure of Russian communism, the Christian variety might have had an easier time of it. Still, by the time that China abandoned the policy of officially favouring atheism in 2053, there had already been multiple generations of Christian families practicing their faith without official clearance from the ruling party.

The effect of such a schooling was dramatic. Firstly the lack of public worship neutered the potential for any form of Christian-related industry to emerge, much as it had in the west. Secondly, the

2099
Rapturists announce Year of Departure

2099
Utah University claims 'cure for ageing'

2100
Rapturist attendance declines

2101
International Air-Highways Act

Church had been forced to favour integration with the local community. Those that retreated were notable by their absence, and frequently singled out. By engaging with their local communities, Chinese Christians were presented with a seemingly unending supply of opportunities to put faith into action and help others that had been overlooked by society. Finally, the Church had become to some extent less bound to Scripture, or at least, less rigid in their approach than evangelical or catholic strands. The reason was simple; Chinese Bible translation was an emerging skill, and it required profound knowledge of the meaning behind the text, rather than just an awareness of the words themselves. And so a culture emerged that valued both Biblical analysis and hermeneutics as well as the continued development of language. In other words, the Bible that the Chinese read changed subtly from generation to generation.

In India, the growth had been similarly dramatic. As the population had risen, so had the proportion of believers in both countries. But while in China the Church had emerged from the underground over the length of an entire century, in India the process had been far quicker. The Christian Social Party – though in no way a theocratic political force – had gained power in 2086, largely thanks to the votes of the Christian-dominated south of the country. There, the Church had been active for years, influencing political decisions and speaking out on behalf of the overlooked among society, but it was only with the outbreak of the Kerala Revival in 2076 that their numbers had grown dramatically.

The revival started not in a church, but an orphanage outside Kochi. Children, cared for by nuns from a forgotten sub-order of the

2103
Malik Dhara shot, confirmed dead, comes back to life

2119
Pilgrims to Yarrabah, Australia top 1 million

2128
First manned mission to Mars

2133
Assassination of Joseph Adam Smith III

Missionaries of Mercy, were discovered praying for a local Hindu Brahmin who had fallen ill and was not expected to recover. Their prayers and his recovery sparked a full-scale riot of interest. Within weeks the Hindu temples were filled with Christians praying and Hindus converting, while a few months later the impact spread north, creating almost overnight a Church of fresh converts and reinvigorated Christians.

Like the Church in China, the Indian revival in Kerala was house-based. Due to increased hostilities and tension Hindu temples ceased to be suitable venues for meetings once it spread out of the tolerant Kerala region. Like China, the meetings were low-key affairs, with an emphasis on Christians becoming active in meeting the needs of their local communities.

And so a new form of Church emerged; the Chinese marked by fresh approach to Scripture and debate, the Indian defined more by its dramatic healings and miracles. Both looked back to a time when the early Church existed and wondered whether this return to the underground might in fact be the beginning of a new phase within the Church, one for which there was good reason to be optimistic.

POTENTIAL FULFILLED

There was good reason for those in the House Church movement to be optimistic. They had successfully navigated their way towards being politically tolerated without giving over power to another Constantine. Also, their ability to allow doctrine to evolve and different expressions to be practiced without splits or fresh denominations occurring as a result, lent them a strong sense of unity. Finally, it was clear that they

2099
Rapturists announce Year of Departure

2099
Utah University claims 'cure for ageing'

2100
Rapturist attendance declines

2101
International Air-Highways Act

were having a dramatic impact upon the world around them.

The gift of a home and protection to those Israelis who survived the 2062 destruction of Israel had proven to the rest of the world that India was not only a leading statesman, but a country whose politics were defined to some degree by a Christian sense of sacrifice and help for those in need. With the arrival of the refugees came a link back to the early roots of Christianity, and though the first steps were tentative, gradually the Jewish and Christian communities within south India had formed close bonds, giving the Church a unique appreciation of the culture into which Jesus had been born.

While there was no overall structure to the Church, different groups within local regions tended to meet together and offer mutual oversight. These 'councils' helped correct issues as they emerged. At times certain individuals tried to wrestle for control, but since the churches employed nobody and had no real assets to speak of, there was little power or money worth fighting over.

The style of meetings varied slightly from group to group, but as a whole they followed the model of the early Church as was vividly depicted by the recreations masterminded by Orthodox filmmaker and theologian, Bartholomew Costas in his 2031 series of short films dramatising the life of early Church fathers like Origen and Tertullian. Such was the interest in the work, that there was a drive among some quarters of the Orthodox Church to create a new apocrypha, including in it the source material for Costas' work.

What lasted, instead of alterations to the canon of Scripture, was a renewed interest in the early years of Christianity. Not that the House Church movement attempted to recreate the days of three-

2103
Malik Dhara shot, confirmed dead, comes back to life

2119
Pilgrims to Yarrabah, Australia top 1 million

2128
First manned mission to Mars

2133
Assassination of Joseph Adam Smith III

year catechists and naked baptisms on Easter morning. The intervening years that spanned the conversion of Constantine and the end of Christendom had sent the growth of a remarkable Church. Just as the Reformation had created a point in the development of theology from which Christians could never truly regress, so too had the work of the Victorian social activists and theologians like Barth and Bonhoeffer brought an understanding of the Church's purpose and status that was impossible to ignore.

The House Church movement grew to accommodate what some might have considered polarising extremes. The approach to Scripture that emerged from China might have at one point been labelled as liberal theology, while India's roots as a nation stirred by miraculous and inexplicable encounters with God's Spirit could easily have led it back towards the heady days of an over-sugared evangelical charismatic movement. Yet the common ground that united them was far firmer than history might have predicted.

Worship within the groups took on a range of forms. Some, like those in the former Russian territories (taken over by China after the Soviet collapse of 2029) leant more towards liturgical sung worship, drawing heavily from their Orthodox tradition. Native Chinese Churches rejected song in large part, opting for a more contemplative approach that some mischievously termed Quaking Christian Buddhism. Others in India found themselves re-absorbing sung worship from African communities as individuals returned from humanitarian work in the continent. Other Indian Christians' worship was distinctly flavoured by the slowly increasing Jewish community among them.

2099
Rapturists announce Year of Departure

2099
Utah University claims 'cure for ageing'

2100
Rapturist attendance declines

2101
International Air-Highways Act

Regardless of structure or style, the Church across the east and south was now dominated less by denomination and more by the flavours of local communities.

Having taken a lead in the malarial missions across Africa, India introduced House Churches to the continent. Basic lack of infrastructure hampered progress, but the Church lobbied hard the governments of the two superpowers to instigate an extensive road building programme in areas that remained undeveloped. Once the people could transport food and energy-generating resources, many of the shantycities began to empty, much as they had already in south India and Thailand. The desperate scramble for life eased for many, and the message of the Church was heard in a thousand whispers: God is not dead.

THE ETERNAL QUESTION

When the Smiths stood on display in 2100, the men flushed with life like a mother holding her hour-old baby, it is said that Europe and America cheered. Africa turned away and wept while China and India wondered how the two would ever be reunited. After centuries of slavery and colonial rule, followed by abandonment and blank stares, Africa's tears at the advances in the LDS were part sorrow, part anger. Talk of white men living for one thousand years filled them with terror, and history was invoked to strengthen their case for opposition.

While Africa raged, India and China attempted to pacify the masses. It was an almost impossible task. The assassination of Joseph Adam Smith III on 17 January 2133 had been a long time coming.

2103
Malik Dhara shot, confirmed dead, comes back to life

2119
Pilgrims to Yarrabah, Australia top 1 million

2128
First manned mission to Mars

2133
Assassination of Joseph Adam Smith III

For years the Churches had preached peace and tolerance, and for years the LDS and its expanded territories had waved its advances under the noses of a world now clearly divided again. As Economy A grew, bringing the northern European and American states even greater wealth and potential to manipulate life as they wished, Economy B struggled to sustain the remaining eighty per cent of the global population.

Little wonder that President (as he was correctly titled) Joseph Adam Smith III was a target. As he stepped onto the stage to address the assembled audience at Cairo University in the winter sun, somehow the security systems failed to pick up the most basic threat of all; Joseph Makwezi, young enough to be Smith's grandson, yet looking older and more weary than his target, rushed the stage and shot him dead.

EVOLUTION

They used to call it the Great War because it was impossible to conceive of any other loss of life on so grand a scale ever taking place again. Thirty years later, it had been renamed, and World Wars I and II were over. The first started with an assassination, the second with the invasion of an innocent country. In the wake of President Smith's assassination in 2133, LDS threatened to attack Uganda – Makwezi's homeland and most vocal critic of LDS. An assassination and an attack of a virtually undefended country. Was the trilogy of war about to be made complete?

Epilogue

2133 – The End of the Beginnng

Last week they started issuing tracking tags to all Christians living in the Atlanta-Five commune. A month ago it was the turn of those living in the Northern Territories. No one really minded or thought to protest that much. It seemed like a sensible precaution to take, but there was a look of fear among the faithful as they opened their doors to the medical police. You could see it on the screen.

The reasons are obvious. In the last three years life has been growing increasingly tense in America. The LDS – who else? – have increased their territory substantially. It started with those Hidden Church protectorates back when our parents were young. The lure of immortality was too much to resist, and bit by bit, the LDS expanded until it spread from the Pacific coast between Ventura and Vancouver over the Rocky Mountains and halfway across the great desert of Kansas and Texas.

That was the start. Then it all got theological. The Doctrine

Wars of the late 2030s were fierce affairs, with constant battles over Mormon and Christian interpretations of Scripture. You used to get into trouble for writing that kind sentence, the type with 'Mormon' and 'Christian' together but referring to the two different groups. A while back they gave up though, the Mormons finally conceding that they were different from non-Mormon Christians after all.

The Trinity was always the big one. No matter how close we could get on justification or salvation, or even on the resurrection and the virgin birth, things always fell apart when it came down to the Holy Spirit. There was no chance of any Rapturists giving it up, and as for the Slow Faith Church, erasing the third person from the Trinity was a complete dead end. So the Doctrine Wars raged on, and every once in a while they would get violent. Bands of suited thugs would attack libraries and schools at night when they were closed. Burning or bombing or sometimes just doing whatever they could to disrupt the next day's activities, they never got caught; the scanners never picked them up.

Everyone knew what was going on, yet what could we do about it? Just like our own atmosphere, we got used to breathing in a compound of influences: part resignation, part fear, part relief that someone was taking control. I suppose that's why I started this, it was my attempt to get something else into my lungs, my reaction against the air. There must be better than this.

When the assassination of President Smith was broadcast, the whole world assumed that it wasn't just Uganda that was going to be 'corrected', but that whole of sub-Saharan Africa. The region had long been a pain to the LDS, threatening, complaining, demanding help at the same time as well as threatening some more.

But the attack never came, and few now think that it ever will. The House Churches have worked hard to bring communities together, to have people focus on the challenges on their doorstep, not across the oceans. It seems to be working.

THE GUESS

So the reason for the tracking tags and the increased scans round here has nothing to do with the Africans. But it is linked to the Church. Ten years ago we started hearing rumours about a girl from Malaysia. Hema Kassipillay was at the centre of reports of a range of miracles. There were stories of healings and changes in the areas where she lived. Some were quick to start talking about the second coming, saying that Jesus was back. But as a woman? It was controversial, although not to me. Why wouldn't he take the form of a woman? Think about it, the main reason for taking male form before was surely to do with the cultural context into which he was being placed. Would a woman have been listened to? Would she have been followed? Would she have been crucified? Today's culture is different, and with the undercurrents of failed masculinity there are plenty around who think that Jesus would be crazy *not to* return as a woman. I imagine there might be some issues with the id change, but surely God could work it out, couldn't he? Whatever the future, at least she made us think, and if Hema had carried on doing all the things that she had been doing then perhaps the idea might have caught on a little more. But she didn't; she just disappeared and nobody has heard of her since.

Still, the Mormons certainly did not like the idea of Christians believing that God would come back as a diminutive schoolgirl from the East. Particularly not when he'd gone to all that bother of being a man the first time around. To prove it, they just happened to have one of their lucky finds again. It turns out that Joseph Smith had already predicted Hema's arrival on the scene, and she would be one of a number of false prophets to surface around the time of the real return.

A few more of these people have emerged over the last few years. They're not all women, but they do all disappear after a while. We've got used to the pattern too, and the Hidden Church seems to be in on the act. The routine is simple; a few people start talking about miracles that occur when a particular person is around them. For a few days we see evidence on screens wherever we look, and then the theologians speak up and declare Malik or Jenna or Senna or Javal or Miros a fraud. They disappear and we all go back to our lives, resetting our optimism back in the trap, ready to be set free the next time it is required.

BELIEF

With Jared Hart it was different. The moment he spoke it was clear that he was a set-up. The others never had me convinced, they always left enough room for doubt. None of them ever looked the same, and they all spoke in different ways, even when you factor out the translation programmes they use for live transmissions these days. But Jared's first footage seemed to try too hard to be random. He always knew where the cameras were, was always audible, was always able to make sure we got a good clear look as he wept or raged or prayed over the body of some supposedly lifeless child.

Anyway, Jared's become the one that we're all supposed to believe in, and he's delivering his first temple address today. What's the bet he pulls out some ancient scroll of Isaiah to read from? It all smacks of farce. Mormons around the west will be going to their nearest local temple to listen, watch and pray together. Their display of unity and fleet-footed hope is a joke. The suits will be watching and anyone who fails to attend will be called to account.

I might watch it. But I know what it'll be like; the screen will be full of Immaculates and the segregated audience will weep at the right times. A girl in a white dress will approach, her limbs atrophied or congenitally malformed thanks to radiation poisoning or some cheap genetic mutation procedure gone wrong. She'll be helped up to the platform and Jared will stop, he will do that thing he does with his eyes and he will place his hands on the limbs. And they will be healed. And in those seconds after the limbs are fully restored – before I gorge myself on cynicism and doubt – I, like pretty much everyone else around here, will want to believe that all these rumours are true.

And when I quit the transmission, I will return to the low-level fear that's everywhere these days. The fear that if we make too much fun out of the LDS they will launch an attack upon us. The fear that I might be wrong about all this. The fear that the Rapturists might be right after all. The fear that somehow, even with a tracking tag now embedded in my cheek, I might end up another victim of the attacks that the state seems unable to stop.

TOMORROW

My writing about fear is a rabbit trail. Don't trust me with it. I'm not really scared about all this. At least, I'm not scared any more. The dry mouth and the awkward guts have shifted, eased and subsided. When I think about Christianity there's a bolder, stronger sensation that settles the twitches down. Why feel scared when so many have been through so much and still the faith continues? Why feel scared when the list of martyrs spans the millennia? Why fear when death by stone or fire or nail or bullet or rope or bomb or toxin can never be the end of the story? I always knew that my death would be just the end of the beginning and that a thousand stories would be written for every day of the life to come. But now my eyes are burning at the thought that death does little to halt the force and momentum of a life lived in pursuit of service of God. Those martyrs may have fainted from the pain and craved the moment their souls moved on to the eternal, but their death did not diminish the impact of their living. Death dies twice for the disciple of God.

We are well used to talking about endings these days. Aren't we all aware of how close we came to destruction in the last century? Whether by our own hands or the consumption of the generations that went before, we were pulled closer to extinction than history could recall. And then there's been the end of culture – or, to be precise, the end of Literate Culture. Perhaps there are so many students with their Second Orality study guides around these days that I'm preaching to the choir here, but it's worth going over the facts just once more:

In the beginning we were oral. We communicated our stories, our values and all the rest by word of mouth and face to face. Stories were central to the process of education, and relationship was inextricably intertwined with understanding; getting to know something and someone were one and the same.

Then things changed. It was that guy with the goose flesh who is probably to blame somehow (remember the Guttenberg story?). With the invention of the printing press and movable type the west became a literate culture. With the mass production of books the way that knowledge was communicated shifted. Soon it was possible for it to be transferred in a method other than person-to-person. Gradually we evolved into something new: a culture that esteemed reason above all else. It was bad news for religions, despite what they said at the time. Literate Culture forever resisted the attempts of the faithful to adopt it as their own. They simply didn't look natural together.

And then, once the technological revolution took place back in the twentieth century, things evolved again. We emerged into a reworked version of the original Oral Culture. We might not be doing it face to face – or, at least, not round some fireside with the stars lighting our gatherings – but we are connected to each other once more. Reason and rationalism have taken a back seat and the strengthening of relationship is once more twinned with the acquisition of knowledge.

Evolution used to be controversial. But not any more. Christians used to try to adopt the tools of science and reason to explain the Bible, but always came up short. These days we're comfortable once more with stories being stories. We've ditched the need for everything to be measurably, empirically true. We're better for it.

It's true that the old Literate Culture of Europe and the west gets a bad press these days. We paint it as lacking integrity, being obsessed with outer conformity at the expense of true inner freedom. We play our part in the Church as well, pining for those early days back when we were an original oral culture. The common assumption is that we began to lose our way when things started getting written down.

But if this project has taught me anything, it is that those sweeping generalisations just aren't what they're cracked up to be. Just look at what happened before and after the Reformation and it's clear that the Church in the oral culture was more than capable to sinking to unfathomable depths, while the most significant episode in the early days of the literate culture – marked with completely literate clarity by a man nailing a long list of statements to a door – ended up being one of our greatest moments.

Christianity's not like that. It's not limited by culture. In fact, we're the only followers of a major religion that doesn't prescribe a set of values that dictate the way we eat, dress or work. It works whatever the backdrop. It has to.

But, stop. I don't want to do this. Not now. I don't want to weigh up, assess or evaluate. I'm done with being that kind of detached observer who watches from the sidelines. Perhaps that's what this work started out as – an attempt to dig and prod and work out if any of this was really worth believing in after all – but it's become so much more than that.

It started with the first pages and I can still feel the adrenaline working now. Highlights? There are too many to mention, but if you were to push me I'd be holding up Aquinas, Bonhoeffer and that Pope who never made it past the first few months. I've got a soft spot for PM Wassim whose open arms welcomed the Jews, and I can't get the thought out of my head that Saladin was a far more godly man than many in the Church would give him credit for. I'll never forget the image of Origen standing half naked and rethinking his desire to become a martyr while the breeze cooled his enthusiasm, and I haven't even told you about Perpetua. You really should look her up for yourself; her sacrifice and integrity cannot fail to inspire.

I have left much out. Time and storage have not allowed me to follow every character and episode that I would have liked to, but then again, how could I have covered it all? By looking at these stories of notable believers I'm now left wondering if it matters less who is remembered through history. Isn't it the small steps that count for more? Isn't it the love, devotion and sacrifice a million times over that we've never heard of that has driven us to where we are? Isn't it all our ancestors that we must thank, not merely those whose names have endured?

Words and things; one and the same. If only we could grasp a little tighter the idea that our every breath, sound and movement adds definition to this story of Christianity. To borrow an image from the old days; the pen rests solely in our own hands.

I am no longer an observer. I am now a participant. I want to write myself into this story, even though I will never get a mention. I want to script myself in with the countless characters whose threads make this story what it is. I want to belong to this, to be consumed by this, to be one more invisible grain of sand that is part of the shore that borders sea and land.

But what next? What about the future? Are we really at the end of the beginning? Is Jared Hart the one, or are there further generations yet to come who will look back and smile at our predictions of immanent endings? I'm only convinced of these two things: that I am less able to predict the end now than I was at the start, and that I am more convinced than ever that whatever follows, we hold the potential to be … to be the sort of Church that God intended. Sacrificial to the point of death, bold to the highest power, serving the ignored, loving in ways that explode all current definitions, sharing without restriction or restraint. We can be even more than this tomorrow.

A Very Selected Bibliography

Robert Atwell, *Spiritual Classics from the Early Church* (The National Society/Church House Publishing, 1995).

Bryan Appleyard, *How To Live Forever or Die Trying: On The New Immortality* (Simon & Schuster, 2007).

Henry Bettenson and Chris Maunder (eds), *Documents of the Early Christian Church*, new edition (Oxford University Press, 1999).

David Chidester, *Christianity, A Global History* (Penguin, 2000).

Eva Haustein-Bartsch, *Icons* (Taschen, 2008).

Jonathan Hill, *The New Lion Handbook of The History of Christianity* (Lion, 2007).

Jonathan Hill, *The History of Christian Thought* (Lion, 2003).

Alan Kreider, *Worship and Evangelism in Pre-Christendom* (Grove Books, 1995).

Joel Marcus, *Jesus and the Holocaust: Reflections on Suffering and Hope* (Doubleday, 1997).

James Martin, *The Meaning of the 21st Century: A Vital Blueprint for Ensuring Our Future* (Eden Project Books, 2006).

Stephen Tomkins, *A Short History of Christianity* (Lion, 2005).